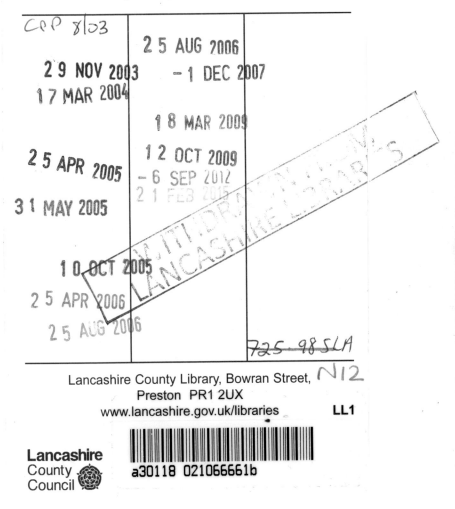

The Bridges of Lancashire and Yorkshire

Birks bridge

The Bridges of Lancashire and Yorkshire

by
MARGARET SLACK

Illustrated by
Kenneth A. Bromley

ROBERT HALE · LONDON

Robert Hale Limited
Clerkenwell House
Clerkenwell Green
London EC1R 0HT

Class 725. 98

British Library Cataloguing in Publication Data

Slack, Margaret
  The bridges of Lancashire and Yorkshire.
  1. Bridges—England—Lancashire—
  History   2. Bridges—England—Yorkshire
  —History
  I. Title
  624'.2'094276   TG58.L3

  ISBN 0-7090-2814-8

Photoset in Palatino by
Derek Doyle & Associates, Mold, Clwyd.
Printed in Great Britain by
St Edmundsbury Press Ltd, Bury St Edmunds, Suffolk.
Bound by Woolnough Bookbinding Ltd.

Contents

To the two Joyces,
Joyce Hemingway
and Joyce Hennessey

Illustrations

Acknowledgements

The author wishes to thank the following people for their help: Mrs D. Burtt, Mrs F. Dinsdale, Mrs J. Ellis, Mrs V. Stark, Mrs J. Vasey, Mr M. Collins for information about packhorse bridges; Mrs B. Brewster, Mr G.A. Leech and Patrick F.-Lombard O.Carm for information about Kettleman's Bridge; Pauline Millward of Bankfield Museum, Halifax, and Mr H.R. Rigg of Towneley Hall Art Gallery and Museums, Burnley, for information about packhorse collars; Mrs D. Loadman of Aldbourne Library, Mr K.H. Rogers, Wiltshire County Archivist and Mr Alan Keen of Aldbourne, for information about packhorse bells; Mrs Boddington of North Humberside County Record Office, Mr M.Y. Ashcroft of North Yorkshire County Record Office; Dave Jowett of Bradford, Mr D. Wood, Principal Engineer of Burnley Borough Council, Miss K. Michaels of the Inland Waterways Association, Mr A.E. Butcher of the Science Museum, South Kensington, for help with civil engineering problems; Mr Dick Capel of Kirkby Stephen; the Reference Librarians of Preston and Lancaster; Miss Jean Siddall and Miss Janice Bell of Burnley Reference Library; Mr J.M. Salmon, Assistant County Librarian, North Yorkshire; Miss Julie McCann, Team Librarian, Selby; Mrs C.E. Vickers, Barnsley Library; Mr D. Hardwick, Rotherham Library.

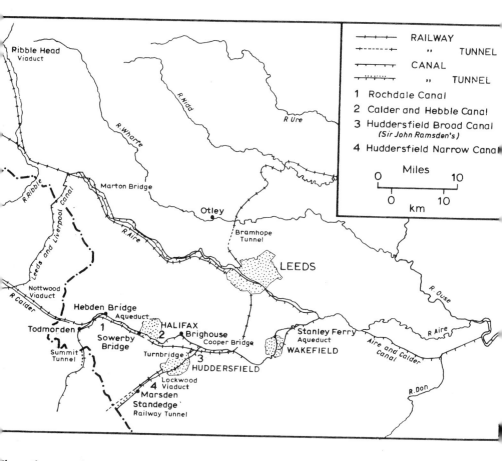

The railway and canal bridges of Yorkshire

The river bridges of Yorkshire

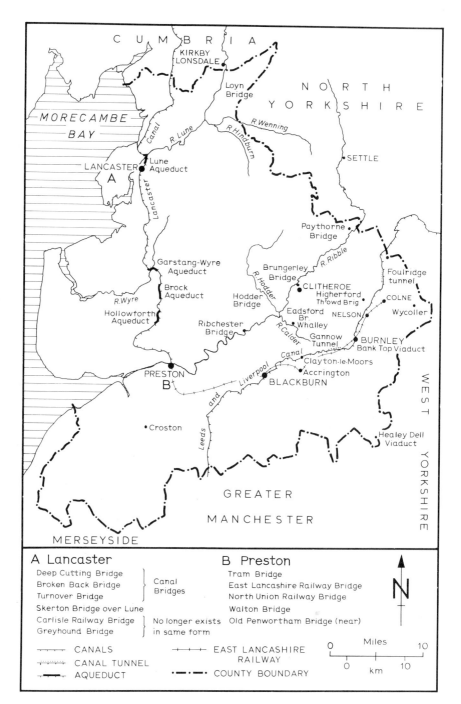

C U M B R I A

KIRKBY
LONSDALE

Loyn
Bridge

N O R T H

Y O R K S H I R E

MORECAMBE
BAY

R. Lune

Canal

R. Wenning

R. Hindburn

• SETTLE

LANCASTER
A

Lune
Aqueduct

Lancaster

Paythorne
Bridge

Garstang-Wyre
Aqueduct

Brock
Aqueduct

Brungerley
Bridge

R. Hodder

R. Ribble

Fouiridge
tunnel

R. Wyre

CLITHEROE
Higherford
Th'owd Brig

Hodder
Bridge

COLNE

Hollowforth
Aqueduct

Ribchester
Bridge

Eadsford
Br.
• Whalley

NELSON

Wycoller

R. Calder

Gannow
Tunnel

BURNLEY
Bank Top Viaduct

Canal

Clayton-le-Moors

Liverpool

• Accrington

PRESTON
B

BLACKBURN

and

• Croston

Leeds

Healey Dell
Viaduct

W
E
S
T

G R E A T E R

M A N C H E S T E R

Y
O
R
K
S
H
I
R
E

MERSEYSIDE

A Lancaster

Deep Cutting Bridge
Broken Back Bridge   } Canal
Turnover Bridge   Bridges
Skerton Bridge over Lune
Carlisle Railway Bridge } No longer exists
Greyhound Bridge   in same form

B Preston

Tram Bridge
East Lancashire Railway Bridge
North Union Railway Bridge
Walton Bridge
Old Penwortham Bridge (near)

---+--- CANALS
············ CANAL TUNNEL
---•--- AQUEDUCT

+---+---+ EAST LANCASHIRE
RAILWAY
-•---•-- COUNTY BOUNDARY

N

Miles
0 ———————— 10
0 ———————— 10
km

The bridges of Lancashire

1 Clapper and Packhorse Bridges

They heard it first; a distant rumbling and roaring like a nameless threat. Then they saw the turbulent brown water whipped into boiling foam, racing down the hillside. Already they were tired from a day hunting and burdened with the weight of the animals they had killed. They had no alternative but to walk several miles to the headwaters of the river and back down the other side.

Probably a tree, blown down by frequent gales and spanning the distance between two banks first suggested to the mind of early man the idea of a bridge. Trees, purposely felled and deliberately placed, enabled him to control his crossing points. To strip the trunk of its treacherous bark and smooth the curved surface into flatness was probably one of the early refinements he made. From this it would not take him long to evolve a crossing with two such tree trunks joined by struts, enabling him to transport animals from one side of the water to the other. This primitive wooden beam bridge although the simplest and no doubt the most common method devised by early man of crossing water, was not the only way. Another, eminently suitable for crossing wider stretches of water was to make a sort of stepping-stone system by means of a series of small boats connected by timber – a pontoon bridge. Or, if light but supple and strong material were available a suspension bridge was made. Suspension bridges were built in ancient China. Man adapted himself to his surroundings and shaped the environment to his way of life. Fallen trees were suitable for crossing streams, pontoon-type bridges for wider rivers or lakes, where, in an economy dominated by water, the possession of a small boat or boats would have been normal.

Where, however, the span of the river was too wide for a single tree, stone piers were built as supports for several tree trunks making a longer beam bridge – the clapper bridge. As early as *c.*

800 BC stone piers were used as supports for a bridge across the Euphrates.

In time man's engineering skill developed the arch bridge, more graceful than the beam bridge and more useful, as there was room for boats to pass under the arch. The Romans were great exponents of bridge building, developing the technique and favouring the use of the semi-circular arch, although there is insufficient evidence to make it certain that they built arched bridges in Britain. One authority thinks that they did. 'Mr Wright says Mr Roach Smith has pointed out a very fine semi-circular arched bridge over the little river Cock near its entrance into the Wharfe, about half a mile below Tadcaster.'[1] Is this, by implication therefore, a Roman bridge? After the dissolution of the Roman Empire bridge building almost ceased in Western Europe for about a thousand years and its revival began in Italy, owing much to the work of Leonardo da Vinci.

Clam bridge, Wycoller

Bridge building was not static; it was not long before man found that wood as a building substance was not really satisfactory; it had a short life, it rotted, it was vulnerable to fire and it was easily washed away by streams in spate. And so stone began gradually to replace wood for building, giving more durability to bridges.

An example of a stone beam bridge is the Clam bridge across the Wycoller Beck at Wycoller in Lancashire. Wycoller is a hamlet which, in the past, depended on farming and the domestic textile industry and is now dependent on farming and tourism. In areas where stone was plentiful such as the Granite moors of Dartmoor, the Gritstone areas of the Mid-Pennines and the Carboniferous limestone of the Craven District of Yorkshire, the supply of material for bridge building presented no problem, although in fact flagstones in Carboniferous limestone are rarely seen in use in clapper bridges. But its quarrying, in one huge slab, dressing – although the Clam bridge is not meticulously or geometrically squared – transporting and placing, represent an enormous task. The present slab on the Clam bridge is probably nineteenth-century and is balanced at a curious angle which makes it look unsafe, although in fact it is quite firm. In order to provide safety in slippery weather or late at night for those who had celebrated well but unwisely, there was, in former years, a handrail fixed at one side and the holes which supported this handrail can still be seen. A similar bridge is one crossing the beck on the way to Windgate Nick, near Addingham, and another, with a squared-and-dressed stone, is that on the footpath from Hanlith to Malham, about a couple of field lengths from the centre of the village. There is also an excellent example at Helwith Bridge in upper Ribblesdale at the bottom of Long Lane. More famous, but possibly more modern, is that at the Brontë waterfalls near Haworth. The slab has been dressed and squared and the wall at either side of the stream built up and stepped outwards across the beck so that the crossing can be made by one slab of stone although there are two approach stones. This is a bridge which was beloved by the Brontë sisters Charlotte and Emily and where Emily, 'half reclining on a slab of stone, played like a young child with the tadpoles in the water.'[2]

An example of a clapper bridge is to be found at Wycoller, nearer the hamlet than the Clam bridge and in a place where the stream is too wide to be spanned by a single flagstone. Dating

Clapper bridge, Wycoller

from the late eighteenth or early nineteenth century, the bridge became so worn with use that it was levelled and made safe by a local farmer.

Fine examples of clapper bridges are those at Crummackdale near Austwick, and at Malham. The situation of the clapper bridge at Crummackdale is different from those at Wycoller and Malham, in that it is not in the centre of the village but on the edge of it and away from the main farms. It provides a convenient and easy crossing for traffic coming north to south on the track which comes from Ribblesdale through Sulber Gate and down Crummackdale. This is a high bleak route crossing a limestone pavement which is quite dry; and as there are no surface streams there is no need for a causey to avoid bog. But there are other hazards; it is real ankle-breaking terrain doubly treacherous in mist where one can easily miss the path. The limestone pavement and outcrops are punctuated in places by grassy strips but in a mist it is not easy to locate these. Crummack farm, just over 900 feet high, is the only house for some distance. The traffic along this track must, in the past, have been considerable, to merit the building here of a substantial bridge.

One of the clapper bridges at Malham crosses the stream by

The Clapper bridges of Malham

Beck Hall linking farms at one side of the village with those at the other side; and another crosses it near Malham Cove. Great labour must have been involved initially in the construction of these bridges. Along with the Gritstone area of the Pennines the limestone uplands of the Craven district are famous for their drystone walling; this said, the achievement of building stone piers durable enough to maintain the weight of the horizontal flagstones and the force of the flowing water for any length of time was not inconsiderable. The largest and arguably the finest of the clapper bridges is Moon bridge, sometimes called Wash Dub bridge, a little higher upstream from Beck Hall, which linked the farms in Malham East with those in Malham West. Here the stream is wide and there is a shallow pool which could, in the past have been used for dipping sheep, so perhaps the name Wash Dub bridge originated from this – but this is purely conjecture. It is probably that at one time the bridge in the village, Monk Bridge, was also a clapper-type bridge, but with the increase in traffic an arched bridge was built, and later widened. It is possible, by looking underneath it to see the structure of the narrow bridge. This single arch bridge was endowed by William Preston of Hill Top who, in 1636, left £6 towards the cost of construction of a one-arch bridge.

In the Colden Valley near Hebden Bridge, just below Jack Bridge is a superb example of a very old stone footbridge, Hebble

Hebble Hole Bridge

Hole Bridge. The horizontal comprises four squared-and-dressed stone slabs something which is not apparent until one actually gets on to the bridge; from the approach it looks as if the horizontal is in a single piece. The structure is supported by an enormous boulder in the stream on which are three deep stone slabs.

There is an excellent example of a clapper bridge at Linton-in-Craven, an illustration of which appears in several of Edmund Bogg's books on Wharfedale. These show the bridge as it was at the turn of the century when many of Bogg's books were written. The bridge has now been removed from its original position, resurfaced with asphalt and provided with a handrail.

Few ordinary people in the Middle Ages travelled far, their journeys mainly being in the immediate neighbourhood of their place of work; from one farm to another; from their cottages to the manor house to attend the manor court; from their farms to worship at church; to the weekly market to buy those commodities they were unable to grow or make at home, or to sell their surplus produce. A journey further afield and an event of great importance was the yearly or half-yearly visit to the fair. Although freer than their rural counterparts to leave home many of the urban craftsmen lived and worked for an entire lifetime in their towns, rarely, if ever venturing from them. So, for them, the existing footpaths and footbridges sufficed.

Nevertheless, a surprisingly large amount of movement did take place in the Middle Ages. Freemen owing suit of court had to attend the manor court and litigants had to appear there; drovers took flocks and herds of animals to market; monks or lay brethren visited their granges and drove their sheep from winter to summer pastures and back again; clergy and church representatives travelled between churches, and itinerant merchants followed recognized routes between fairs. Chapmen, badgers, hucksters and pedlars supplied a need by taking their wares to scattered houses and farms.

The routes used by these travellers nearly all crossed the high ground, there were tracks which breasted the hills, going from one valley to the next, and there were 'middle ways' which snaked along the contours overlooking the valley but keeping just below the high moorland in the lee of the hill. The method of transit was on foot or by horseback, goods being taken by means of trains of packhorses, packhorse travel developing when the monastic houses were in their heyday. For the monasteries, although they had been founded for the worship of God and the furtherance of spiritual activity were at the same time great busines centres.

Like Topsy, their power and business influence 'just growed' and as each Order in time outgrew its pure spirituality, another was founded the better to focus the attention of the monks on their vows of poverty, chastity and obedience. Many of the Orders were based on the Rule of St. Benedict who believed that to work was to pray. The monastic houses therefore were self sufficient; the monks, or, more likely, the lay brethren, who also lived there, practised, among other trades, pottery, leather-working, and textile manufacture. As the years passed bequests from those who wished to ensure for themselves a good seat in the kingdom of heaven meant that they in time became landowners on a considerable scale. Not only did the monks farm land they also exploited the minerals which lay beneath it so that eventually they became great agriculturalists and industrialists. The wide open spaces and the rolling hills of the Pennine country and the Yorkshire moors were ideally suited to sheep-farming and, in the Middle Ages, the Cistercian Monks of Yorkshire produced and sold great quantities of wool. This, and also iron ore, was taken by packhorse from the various granges to the Mother house and hence to its ultimate destination.

Packhorse travel, which was not distinctive to Lancashire and Yorkshire was the usual form of transport for five centuries. It was not used exclusively by monks, there were lay as well as monastic industrialists; nor was it used solely for the transport of wool and iron ore; coal, peat, lime, lead, hides, charcoal, finished cloth and corn were taken by packhorse. Ladies were sometimes conveyed in this way to London from the north, one young lady being reckoned in weight to equal half a pack.

There were various methods of fitting loads onto packhorses. An illustration in Walker's *The Costume of Yorkshire* would seem to suggest that the pieces of cloth were just slung over the backs of the horses without any fastening. In fact they would probably be secured with a leather strap or belly-band to which was attached a long rope, the fitment being known as a wanto, wanty or wanter. There were load saddles, some with a wooden crutch or a ledge; some saddles were padded, some unpadded. To these saddles, depending on the goods to be carried, wicker pannier baskets were attached, some of the baskets had hinged bottoms to allow them more easily to be unloaded, the coal, lime or whatever, simply dropping out. The normal load was about $2\frac{1}{4}$ hundredweight.

Packhorses travelled in trains of twenty to forty animals with a driver and one or two attendants. The leading animals would wear a collar with bells each with a different note indicating by its tone to animals further back in the train and to approaching traffic whether the train was turning left or right. Not so very many years ago a common game among children was 'bell horses'.

There were many hazards of packhorse travel one of which was being bogged down in a sea of mud. The swampy peaty country of the high Pennine moorlands is difficult to negotiate after prolonged rain; churned by the feet of horses it would be diabolical. A way of getting over this difficulty was to build a paved track or causey (causeway) slightly raised above the ground. This provided a firm surface although the narrowness and height of the causey above the ground level could prove a nuisance and also, on occasion, a danger. One can imagine the difficulties if two trains of packhorses met head on, and the altercations between the drivers. And of course packhorse traffic was not the only traffic using the tracks.

One traveller was Oliver Heywood the famous seventeenth-century Divine from Calderdale. He relates a misadventure of which he was a witness.

> As I was riding by Brighouse Nov. 1 1680, I met a man on an horse and driving two horses before him with pack-saddles on, yet empty. He had tied them together with an halter. Now just as I met him there was a deep hollow way below and an high Causey above, and the one of the horses took the higher, and the other the lower way. It was impossible that the lower should leap up to the other and there was great hazzard of the higher falling, and both ways they could not go for the distance was beyond the reach of the halter … At last the man fearing the issue light off his horse and run towards the lower horse to pull off the halter; but as he ran the horse in the hollow way leapt up with his fore feet to mount the Causey, but not being able, fell down and pulled the other backwards after him. With the fall was a crashing noise. I made account that the horse's back or neck had been broken, for there lay the horse with his feet upwards and stirred not … However there was no hurt except for two bakestones on the horse that fell which were masht to pieces and the man made great lamentation for the breach of the Baking Stones.[3]

Many of the packhorses used in the north of England were

imported from Germany and were known as Jaegar ponies (hunter ponies). It is from this that place names including the word Jagger originate – Jagger Lane, Jagger Hill and so on, which are to be seen in parts of the north. Edmund Bogg in several of his topographical books has an illustration of a packhorse train which is labelled Jagger ponies. Galloways were also used, they were common in Calderdale.

Many of the tracks can still be seen; many more have been metalled and are now used as motor-roads. One of the most famous is the packhorse route from Marsden at the head of the Colne valley, Th' Owd Gate. This was not a regular route which was frequented by trains of packhorses but served the local people. It is also known as Eastergate. I was told by a local resident that this was because the snow which invariably blocked the way during the winter months had usually cleared by Easter when the way was open again. Easter being a movable feast this may or may not have been so and in any case this criterion could have been used for all northern packhorse routes. The name in fact derives from a woman, Esther Schofield, who kept an inn called the Packhorse Inn.

Much of the information about the use of the route comes from the writings of the Lancashire author Edwin Waugh who described a man called Old Lame Luke O' Marsden who, in the early years of the nineteenth century served the country grocers in the Failsworth area of Manchester with meal and flour which he had brought from his corn shop in Marsden. On his return journey he loaded his animals with coal if anyone wanted it. Much more information about the route and its use comes from the account of the proceedings of a case held at the Spring Assizes in Leeds in 1908 when, in order to examine the question of a public right of way along the route, the case of the Lord of the Manor v. Marsden Urban District Council was heard. One of the witnesses said she knew of Luke Brierley and she herself had used the road all her life. She said her mother, who was born about 1788, had been able, in still clear weather, to hear the bell horses coming down from the tops. Many other old Marsden residents testified to the use of the road. One produced a packhorse bell which had been in her family for generations. On it were inscribed the letters G.W., G for go and W for whoa.

Now the packhorse way is signed with a tastefully designed oak signpost both at the Marsden end and its junction with the

Close Gate Bridge, Marsden. Also known as Eastergate Bridge

Buckstones Road. It is well marked and snakes across the moorland being routed higher than the headwaters of the tributary streams avoiding the necessity for more bridges. Every so far there is a guidepost with the information P.H. Road. At the Marsden end there is a graceful and pleasing single-arched bridge which crosses the stream; at the Buckstones end (although the packhorse way continues further) there is a wooden beam bridge built for the use of walkers on the Pennine Way, as the two tracks reach Buckstones road at almost the same point.

The Pennine Dales are rich in their heritage of packhorse bridges; hump-backed and often rising quite steeply from either end with the parapets deliberately quite low in order to accommodate the panniers or packs. There was no necessity for a packhorse, or any other sort of bridge to have a parapet; some didn't, but there were so many accidents that eventually parapets were built. And with the coming of the turnpikes when the packhorse tracks across the high ground were gradually deserted in favour of the more substantial roads and wider bridges in the valleys, in fact when packhorse trains themselves had become an anachronism, the parapets were not necessarily kept in repair. In

Th'Owd Brig, Higherford

some cases the bridges were demolished. In 1778 the packhorse bridge over Hawksworth Beck was replaced by a new and wider one. It was not until 1859 that Stirk Bridge, which carried the packhorse route from Sowerby to Norland, was demolished. The old bridges had occasional use as foot-bridges, many, especially those in the more remote valleys only coming into their own again in comparatively recent days with the popularity of rambling and pony-trekking. Some bridges in their heyday carried the great packhorse trade routes, others, although technically packhorse bridges would serve to connect a farm or group of farms with a main packhorse artery of trade. There are several such bridges in Upper Calderdale between Mytholmroyd and Todmorden.

One of the most attractive bridges in the two counties is that at Higherford near Nelson, at one time a very important trade link, standing as it does on the direct line of the Roman Road from Castercliffe to Ribchester. It was crossed by teams of packhorses bringing coal from Coal Pit Lane near Gisburn and was also used by lime girls from Lothersdale bringing lime into the district. There has been some dispute about the date of the bridge but it is almost certainly late sixteenth century and it is quite possible that it was built by Squire Bannister of Park Hill. A reference in 1583 is to the Newbrigge of Barrowforde between Parkhill and Whitelee. In the Public Record Office there are extracts from Pleadings in the Duchy of Lancaster. In one, under the date 1591 appears the phrase, '... and alsoe in le overbarroweforthe neare or beneathe the stone bridge late buylded in le overbarroweforthe within the forreste or chaice of Pendle.'[4] There was, at one time, a plate and hook under the bridge which, it was stated, carried a bell to give warning when a flood was coming. This bridge is now referred to as Th' Owd Brig. New in the sixteenth century it could not possibly cope with the volume and weight of the traffic of later centuries; a new bridge and a new road were made which carry the modern traffic and Th' Owd Brig is used by foot passengers and perhaps ponies.

Less graceful in appearance and spoilt aesthetically because of its wooden parapet is Beckfoot Bridge, Bingley. Situated at the foot of Harden Beck, hence its name, it was once on the route used by the monks of Rievaulx Abbey from their Mother house to their iron works at Harden. More importantly this road was the old bridle and packhorse route to and from Bingley for centuries before the Aire bridge was made at Cottingley. It was the main highway through Bingley from Scotland and Cumberland,

Beckfoot Bridge

through Craven to the south of England. For centuries Beckfoot had been spanned by a series of wooden bridges but in 1723 a stone bridge was built. The two masons responsible, Ben Craven and Joshua Scott were paid the sum of £10 for building it. In addition, and for no extra payment, they promised 'joyfully and severally to uphold and keep the sd. Bridge in good and sufficient repair during the terms of seaven years from the day hereof.'[5]

There are other packhorse bridges in the South Pennine area which were, at one time on very important roads. One of these is that at Catlow Bottom near Nelson. In times past the highway

Lumb Bridge,
Crimsworth Dean

from Colne to Burnley and the highway from Clitheroe to Halifax passed across this bridge.

Upper Calderdale was one of the most important areas for the production of woollen cloth and there was considerable trade between the area and the market towns of Yorkshire and Lancashire. A well used packhorse track went from Hebden Bridge up the opposite hillside through Beaumont Clough, snaking along the bottom of the Stoodley Pike hillside to join the track coming from Mankinholes and over the shoulder of the hill into Cragg Vale, and ultimately to Rochdale. This track is little used now except by walkers and pony-trekkers but the small, although substantial bridge in Beaumont Clough remains, without a parapet. In the other direction, towards Burnley, which was an important market town, a route led from Hebden Bridge, through Heptonstall and Colden: this road is now metalled and is known as the old road to Burnley. Near, although not part of this track, is Strines bridge, Strine being another word for stream, which crosses Colden Beck, enabling people from Colden dale to join the main route. It is now a foot-bridge kept in a good state of repair and part of the old causey remains.

Bigger, wider and altogether more substantial is Lumb bridge in

The packhorse bridge, Hebden Bridge

Stainforth Bridge, Ribblesdale

Crimsworth Dean, its fine strong arch giving an indication of the amount of traffic it at one time carried. This bridge lies on one of the packhorse routes from Hebden Bridge to Keighley and Burnley.

Arguably the finest of the packhorse bridges in the Calder Valley and perhaps in the whole of the county is that at Hebden Bridge. The bridge over the Hebden Water, conveniently near the manorial corn mill was the crossing point for clothiers bringing their pieces to be fulled at the fulling mill in the valley and eventually the finished pieces to market, and for the tenants who brought their corn to be ground at the manorial mill – the eastern arch of the bridge spans the tail goit of the bridge mill which was originally the corn mill of Wadsworth. The bridge was built about 1510 and replaced a medieval bridge made of timber. Although it has been extensively repaired, in 1602 and 1657 for instance, it has been neither widened nor rebuilt since its erection. In 1845 the parapet was repaired and was raised in 1890. There are two triangles to enable pedestrians to rest in safety, at the south side, and one at the north.

Standing in splendid isolation near Eastwood is a bridge which appears from the 6 inch OS map to be nameless. It is situated between the cricket pitch at Eastwood and the Rochdale canal, very near to Holmcoat canal bridge. At the other side of the cricket pitch is the busy A646 Burnley road. The bridge, a relic of former days, is trapped between two great arteries of traffic built in later days, the canal, which at one time carried goods across the Pennines, and the modern main road to Lancashire. It looks so fragile one wonders how ever it has stood the test of time.

The bridge in the centre of Marsden village, now a foot-bridge, was probably used at one time to enable the tenants to bring their corn to the manorial mill which was situated not far away.

North Ribblesdale had a considerable amount of packhorse traffic across the valley, with routes from west to east and from south to north. Stainforth bridge is situated on what was probably a Roman road which ran from the camp at Smearsett over Malham Moor and into Wharfedale. There was, until well into the nineteenth century, an important market for corn and oatmeal at Gearstones. The date of its origin appears not to be known and it was evidently held by immemorial usage. As many as twenty to thirty wagons laden with oatmeal came out of Wensleydale which went to supply all the farmhouses for a good many miles around. Preceding the era of farm carts and wagons the meal would be carried by trains of packhorses. Ling Gill

Ling Gill Bridge

bridge carries the track, now the Pennine Way, which would at one time have been an important route to and from Gearstones. This bridge appears to have been rebuilt soon after the new turnpike roads through Craven were completed and bears the inscription 'This bridge was repayred at the Charge of the whole West Rideing anno 1765'. There is a smaller bridge at Thorns Gill and another at Yockenthwaite in Wharfedale which gave connection for traffic coming north from the eastern part of the county.

The most interesting bridge in the two counties, with its tipsy arch giving an impression of imminent collapse, is that at Wycoller. This way of building is one method of reducing pressure from the bank and was quite deliberate. A Ministry of Works Report of 1948 states, 'At first glance this appears to be in a precarious state but it is considered mainly an optical effect due to the extraordinary method employed in springing the arch (entirely of long stones) direct from the rock without any attempt to level it first; the distortion of the arch does not appear to be a recent fault and in fact may never have been true. The bridge is not falling over as appearances suggest'. The bridge is thought to have been built in the thirteenth-century but may have been built in the fifteenth. The voussoirs in the arch extend the complete

Packhorse bridge, Wycoller

The World's End Bridge, Sowerby

width of the bridge making it a remarkable construction in another way. The bridge is referred to as Sally's bridge because tradition has it that a lady of that name was responsible for it being built.

The packhorse bridge near Askrigg, Bow bridge, was built in the first instance by the monks of Fors Abbey which was founded by Cistercian monks and was situated a mile to the west of Askrigg on the road to Hardraw. The monks however, did not survive long in this place but found a much better and more fertile site at *Jervaulx* in Wensleydale where they removed about 1156. There is now nothing remaining of Fors Abbey although the monks for some time maintained a grange there.

The packhorse bridge at Wath in Nidderdale is said to have been built prior to the opening of the burial ground in connection with the chapel at Middlesmoor, its main purpose being to enable corpses to be carried across the river at this point *en route* for burial at Kirkby Malzeard parish church.

At Sowerby near Thirsk is a place called World's End – at one time there was there an inn, now closed, so named by its owner, who built it about the year 1832 because when the Codbeck was in flood people could not get any further that way. The packhorse bridge on the Codbeck was built in 1672 with a grant of £10. Until 1929 the only way into Sowerby from the south was over this bridge or through the ford.

There is no reason why a packhorse bridge should have been an arched bridge rather than a hebble bridge (a footbridge formed from flat slabs of stone) but the use of an arch in bridge architecture gave more scope to the builder. There is also the possibility, especially since many of the packhorses bridges were built to cross moorland streams, that the use of an arch allowed for the rapid and considerable rise of the water and the speed of its movement during periods of heavy rain. It would have been much more difficult to raise a hebble bridge sufficiently to avoid a swift torrent.

Bridge building, as any other aspect of architecture, followed fashion and many of the packhorse bridges are similar. Those at Stainforth, Ivelet (in Swaledale), Birstwith, Linton-in-Craven, Higherford, Sowerby (near Thirsk), Dob Park, have a high arch with a slim graceful elegance and a pleasing symmetry. Smaller, although symmetrical and having rather less grace and elegance are those at Park Mill, near Clayton West, Eastergate and Strines. That in Beaumont Clough is sturdy and substantial and so is that at Catlow Bottom, which has an unconscious air of superiority with its battlemented parapet. One can almost endow them with an individuality. Hebden is unique with its three arches, its cutwaters dividing the currents and its triangles, bigger than any of the others. But it is Lumb bridge with its homely sturdiness which is my favourite.

The usual practice with packhorse bells seems to have been to have the leading animal in the train wear a collar, but in the illustration 'The Pack Horse Convoy' which has been reproduced by several of the older authors, Samuel Smiles is one and Edmund Bogg is another, the leading horse wears a single bell and most of the other animals are bedecked with a hoop of bells. Minding a team of packhorses, even if there were several attendants must have been a very lonely occupation, even though the various teams would frequently cross or converge. The tinkling of bells would have been company, especially so in the awesome silence and stillness of the hills. They would also have given ample warning to other trains in the area of the proximity of the animals. But, unless some definite note was to be determined the hoop of bells would have been little use as an indication of direction.

Probably in the early days of packhorse traffic the bells were made by the monastic house. Perhaps even during monastic times, and certainly after their decline, they were made by tinkers or itinerant craftsmen. But bell-making was also a settled trade. At Market Lavington, in Wiltshire, a county famous for its bell foundries, potters manufactured sheep bells. In the third quarter of the nineteenth century a James Potter at Great Cheverell made small bells, while as late as the early twentieth century a William Lancaster, also of Great Cheverell made sheep and cattle bells.

Principally the fame of the Wiltshire foundries has been achieved through making church bells. The bell-founders were not such exclusively, they carried on other occupations, William and Robert Cor were wooden button-makers, Edward Read and Robert Wells were fustian-makers and James Wells was a corn dealer.

William and Robert Cor had a foundry in the grounds of Court House, Aldbourne, certainly from 1694, and possibly earlier. This was continued until 1724 after which time it was carried on, until 1741, by other members of the family. After 1741 bell-founding was continued there by John Stares and Edward Read, until about 1760 when Robert Wells took over the foundry. Much of his work was concerned with the production of church bells although advertisements of his firm which appeared in local journals in Reading, Oxford and Marlborough, between 1767 and 1772 show that he produced different types of bells. One advertisement which appeared in the *Marlborough Journal* of 6 June 1772 reads:

At the BELL FOUNDRY at Aldbourne, Wilts., CHURCH BELLS are cast in a most elegant and as musical a manner as in any part of the Kingdom, the Founder having made the Theory of Sounds as well as the nature of Metal his Chief Study; Also hangs the same, finding all materials on a complete and concise manner; And also Hand bells prepared and strictly in Tune in any Key. Horse bells, Clock and Room Bells, the neatest of their several Kinds. Likewise Mill Brasses cast and sold at the lowest Prices. All orders will be punctually observed by ROB. WELLS, Founder. He gives Ready Money and his best Prices for Bell Metal.

Wigan was also, apparently a centre of bell-founding. The bells reached parts of the country far removed from their centres of origin. In Bankfield Museum in Halifax there was a packhorse collar with a set of four bells, the fifth being missing; on one of the bells is inscribed the initials G.T., Wigan, while the other three have the initials R.W., apparently the work of Robert Wells.

Towneley Hall Art Gallery and Museum, near Burnley, has an

Packhorse travel

even better example of a packhorse collar. This consists of five bells attached to a leather strap measuring 6 inches by 39 inches. There are two closed bells marked R.W., two closed bells marked C.T. and in the centre an unmarked open bell. They are said to date from about 1753 and to have been used on the packhorse trail from Manchester to Newcastle upon Tyne. If, however, the bells marked R.W. are those of Robert Wells they must have dated from later than 1753.

The closed, spherical shaped bells are known as crotal or 'Rumbler' bells and are the most interesting and beautiful of the small bell types. They were cast in thirty different sizes.

2　Road Bridges

If, as has been claimed, the development of bridge building reflects the progress of civilization, certainly the intricacies of bridge administration reflect the human character, because all of life is there. The piety of some who gave financial help in the form of gifts and bequests for the repair and maintenance of bridges was genuine and sincere. But others may have been inspired less by altruistic motives than by a need for the assurance of a tolerable future both in this world and the next.

The reluctance of villagers to pay for the upkeep of bridges they rarely used was understandable, particularly east of the Lancashire border where one of the more prominent characteristics is the wish to get value for money. So they hung on, hoping that an adjoining parish would pay up.

At worst there were always the tactics of delay – the assumed ignorance of where responsibility lay for the repair of a particular bridge. And at best, having won the right of exemption from the onus of contributing to the cost of bridge repair, to stick, with hard-faced determination, to that privilege. And there were the system-beaters, those who sought to avoid toll by fording the river rather than cross the bridge and the rogues who paid their masons short, or not at all, until a court order was issued.

In the Middle Ages bridgemaking and maintaining was held to be a duty of piety and sanctity; in fact as early as the seventh century the repair of bridges was placed among the *Trinoda Necessitas*, the three burdens of paramount necessity. In centuries in which people had no truck with egalitarianism it was held to be one of the charities owed by the rich to the poor. There was no English equivalent of the French Bridge Friars but indulgences were granted to those who contributed to bridge building and repair – crossing rivers was after all a dangerous business. Many bridges were built with triangular recesses in

Kildwick Bridge

which travellers could rest in comparative safety.

The monasteries which owned vast tracts of land in the north of England built, and usually maintained bridges, particularly those which were on the route between the Mother house and their various granges and other enterprises. Monastic bridge building and maintenance may have been less inspired by piety than by the practical necessity of keeping the wheels of ecclesiastical and business life in motion.

Kildwick Bridge, which must be one of the oldest in the north of England and certainly the oldest over the River Aire, owes much to the canons of Bolton Priory who, in 1305, have this entry in their account book, 'in the building of the bridge of Kyldwyk £21 12s 9d.'[1] The work of the canons is still apparent; the western side which consists of two rounded and two pointed arches all with ribbed understructure, is the work of 1305. Abutting the groins is later work of dressed stone which was put there when the bridge was widened by the County in 1780.

It is likely that the bridge in Malham village was built by

monks or lay brothers of Fountains Abbey or Bolton Priory either separately or jointly as both houses held land in Malham; Fountains Abbey possessed most of the manor of Malham west while Bolton had a principal house for the Prior at Prior Hall.

Bow Bridge, near Askrigg, was built by the monks of Fors and a bridge over the Rye at Helmsley was the work of the monks of Rievaulx. The monks of Whalley Abbey encouraged bridge building and it is probable that the de Lacis who owned vast tracts of land in both Yorkshire and Lancashire encouraged their tenants to build and maintain bridges. The de Lacis, also Lords of the Honour of Pontefract, probably bore the cost of building the early bridges at Castleford and Ferrybridge.

There were also private benefactors. In 1502 Dame Joan Chamberlain, a rich and pious lady of York, at one time married, but who took the veil on her husband's death, left money in her will as follows – Her place in Hundgate has to be sold and the money disposed of for the good of her soul, 'that is to say to the exhibicion of pure chylder apte to lerne at scoles, pore maydens well disposyd to mariages and to wayes or briges broken or hurte to the neuance or nuertie of Cryston people amendynge and reparinge.'[2]

In 1485 Dame Margaret Pygot left twenty shillings 'To the reparacion of the Northbrig' (Ripon).[3] In 1461 Sir John Headlam of Nunthorpe in Cleveland willed, 'To Levynbrig vjs viijd; to Stanebrig be yonde Stokeslay vjs viijd; to the brige be twene Aton and Nunthorp vjs viijd.'[4] The Headlams possessed extensive estates in the Bishopric of Durham.

Henry Saville, one of the younger sons of Sir John Saville Knt. of Thornhill, was one of the yeomen of the King's Chamber; he made bequests for the benefit of bridges in the lower Calder Valley (Yorkshire). In 1483 money was willed thus; 'To the reparacion of Eland brig vjs viijd; of Cowford brigge vjs viijd; of the new brigge called Mirfield brige vjs viijd.'[5] The significance of the amount of six shillings and eightpence is that one of the units of currency in the Middle Ages was the mark, which was worth 13/4; 6/8 therefore was half a mark.

Early in the reign of Edward I Henry de Blackburn left the sum of two shillings per year for the repair of Sawley Bridge. In 1368 a wealthy and pious yeoman of Lancashire, one Thomas del Bothe, left £30 'To the bridge at Salford to be paid in the next three years by equal portions and also five marks yearly for the next ten

Hodder Bridge: known as Cromwell's bridge

years.'[6] In 1428 Henry de Rishton of Dunkenhalgh left 6/8 for the repair of Holt Bridge which is on the highway between Rishton and Clayton-le-Moors. In 'The Spending of the Money of Robert Nowell the sum of 3/4 was given towards the poor in Sabden and 'towards the mending of Sabden Bridge'. An additional sum of 10/- was given 'to the Collectors towards the building of Hodder Bridge.'[7]

Catterick Bridge

It was common for church guilds to build and maintain a bridge in their native town, undertaking to keep watch over it and keep it clean. They had their own chapel which they generally built upon the bridge or at the bridge end. Here they joined together in certain devotions, heard their rules read to them, collected alms for the sick and poor and prayed for absent or deceased brethren. It was usual to leave such a chapel open during the day.

There were also chantry chapels on bridges as well as in cathedrals, monasteries and parish churches. A chantry chapel

Eadsford Bridge

was built or endowed in order that in it masses may be said for the soul of the founder; among the founders being kings, archbishops, bishops, noblemen, priests and wealthy laymen. On Catterick Bridge there was a chapel dedicated to Saint Anne. It was served by a priest from the neighbouring hospital of St. Giles for the benefit of travellers who were expected to contribute to the alms box which was kept for the purpose of collecting contributions towards the maintenance of the bridge. Although in ruins it was still there in 1784 but when the bridge was widened in 1792 it was destroyed. Bridges in York, Sheffield, Leeds, Bradford and Bolton (near Bolton Priory) also, at one time, had chapels. In one of the houses near Bolton Bridge was, as late as 1890, a beam which bore the inscription,

> Thou yat passes by this way
> One Ave Maria here yow say[8]

Sometimes the chapel was built at an approach to the bridge as at Helmsley, and on the bridge over the Ribble at Clitheroe and that over the Ribble at Walton. In 1365 John the Hermit of Singleton had licence to have Divine Service in the chapel at the foot of Ribble Bridge at the Walton side of the river, for three years. The chapel of St. Nicholas at Eadsford which stood on the Yorkshire side of the bridge was erected and endowed with lands at some time earlier than 1211. Chapels remain on the bridges at Wakefield and Rotherham.

One of the duties which was undertaken by the members of the church guilds was to keep watch on the bridge they funded. Watch duty was important and, in the absence of church guildsmen it was the duty of the constable to see that this was done. Situated as they are, at important river crossings bridges are key factors in communication and at times of local or national crisis it was important to control traffic in and out of a town.

1665 is remembered as the year of the Great Plague, but plague was endemic in the centuries before advances in medical science and greater appreciation of the importance of cleanliness had combined to eradicate it. The years 1597 and 1598 were plague years in Craven and in 1598 a special order was issued by the West Riding Justices, as follows, 'In regard to the p'sent sickness in the North country. Yt is ordered that ev'ry Constable w'thin this division shall sett 2 or three to watche and warde within their

Walton Bridge

Sowerby Bridge

Constabulary, and shall see the same dulie kept as well in townes as hamletts. And that from henceforthe household'rs themselves shall keep the watche and ward accordinge to their course and not hirelynges as heretofore hath been accustomed.'⁹

In 1645 a watch-house was built on the bridge at Sowerby Bridge and in 1677, about the time of the Popish Plot we read that five shillings was paid to John Wood being 'his hyre for one yeare warding att Sowerby Bridge.' Again in 1745, at the time of the Jacobite Rebellion the watch was reinforced. In October of that year 10d was spent in setting watch and ward at Sowerby Bridge and Turnpike. The following month 4/6 was paid for three watch bills (billhooks) and 7d for two watch sticks. In January the following entry appears, 'Paid for use of Watch House 10 weeks at 3d ... 2/6.' Every effort was made to see that the watchmen were comfortable, 'Paid for 19 load of coles to Sowerby Bridge Watch at 8d ... 12/8.'¹⁰

Early bridges were made of timber; in fact as late as the seventeenth century Mytholmroyd Bridge was made of wood and in 1659 the Constable was buying timber and a tree for its repair. The bridge over the Lune at Lancaster was also made of wood as late as 1654 and, partially so thirty years later.

In the sixteenth century economic life began to expand and

there was a need for more durable bridges, gradually stone began to replace wood as a building material. Apart from any practical consideration, the lack of stone bridges might have been interpreted as a mark of poverty, whereas their presence seemed to indicate prosperity. Prosperous clothiers bequeathed money for the repair of the highways, and, more frequently, for the repair of bridges in stone. In 1477 John Naylor of Heptonstall bequeathed 4d, 'to the reparacion of the bridge at Heptonstall.'[11] In 1508 began a series of requests for the building of this bridge in stone. Wm. Grenewod of Heptonstall left, 'To the fabric of Hepden bridge 13/4 if those nearest it will build it of stone.'[12] In 1518 Richard Stanclyffe of Halifax bequeathed, 'to the byldyng of Luddyngden brige XL [£10] if so be they take upon hand to bilde the brigge of Stone.'[13]

However the supply of timber was not inexhaustible. In the seventeenth century when it was reported that Gargrave Bridge was ruinous the surveyor said it would be necessary to rebuild it in stone 'which must of necessity be soe because there is noe tymber in that parte of the country fitt for that worke.'[14]

Expansion of trade and commerce was not the only change wrought by the sixteenth century. The decay of the feudal system removed the despotism of the manorial lord; it also removed any benevolence which might have been associated with it. The near demise of the monasteries and the guilds accomplished by Henry VIII and his son, Edward VI, removed two of the agencies which had provided and maintained bridges. The parish succeeded the manor as a unit of administration while there remained the larger areas, the Wapentake in Yorkshire and the Hundred everywhere else; and the County. In 22 Henry VIII (1530-31) an Act was passed which empowered the Justices of the Peace to 'enquire into all manner of annoyance of bridges broken in the highways to the damage of the kings liege people,'[15] to estimate the cost of repair or replacement and levy the cost on the appropriate district.

The procedure was not swift. When a bridge was thought to be in a dangerous state application was made to the Justices accompanied by a statement to the effect that the bridge was 'ruinous and in great decay.'[16] A petition was presented to the Grand Jury at Quarter Sessions when the constables humbly petitioned the 'Right Worshipful his Majesties Justices of the Peace'[17] informing them that the bridge was dilapidated. They humbly begged that the Justices would be pleased to appoint

Wetherby Bridge

some person or persons to survey the ruins, assess the damage and ultimately make some financial contribution to defray the cost of repair.

The petition received, the JPs would then approach two of the local gentry, also magistrates, with the request that they should ask skilled workmen, usually masons, to assess the cost of repair or rebuilding and to send the certificate to the next Quarter Sessions. It was usual for the Justices to give permission for the levying of the sum and also usual for them to appoint at least two supervisors of the work.

The sum levied would be on the parish, or, where a bridge was on a boundary, on the two parishes sharing the common boundary. The constables who had petitioned the distant JPs for help in bridge repair often found it more difficult to wring money from their ever present fellow parishioners; tax collectors in any day and age have never been the most popular members of society. The temptation not even to bother was strong; there was considerable slackness in the collection and disbursement of monies in which case the aggrieved party or parties had recourse to Quarter Sessions. For instance a complainant, Arthur Preston, stated at the Quarter Sessions held at Wetherby in 1599 that in spite of repeated requests he had not been paid £4 13s 4d which was owing to him for the repair of Wetherby Bridge. He further claimed that the money had not been collected. Quarter Sessions ordered that £5 should be levied in Claro Wapentake along with the assessment for Tadcaster Bridge (already overdue) and given to Arthur Preston, at the same time assuring that he promised to 'repaire and sufficiently mend the decaies of the said Bridge at Wetherby.'[18] There were other temptations to avoid payment. Those who brought the decayed bridges to the notice of Quarter Sessions were often careful to plead ignorance as to which parish was responsible for their maintenance and to leave it to the Justices to decide.

From Summerbridge, in Nidderdale, a road led across Dacre pasture to Thornthwaite and from there to West End in Thruscross, where it crossed the River Washburn at Mill Bridge and proceeded over the moor to Bolton Bridge. Mill Bridge was kept in repair by the inhabitants of the township of Thruscross and on 8 July 1658 the constable of Thruscross was ordered to levy 46/8 equally on the inhabitants for the repair of the bridge. This was evidently ignored as six months later a further order was issued with the threat of a £10 fine for non payment.

Subsequent damage to the masonry must have been neglected as just over twenty years later (July 1680) they were again indicted for non repair of the bridge. Apparently this also was ignored and the fabric deteriorated so much that two years later they petitioned the Justices stating that the Mill Bridge was in ruin and they were unable to repair it. A further two years elapsed before, (July 1684), a fine of 30/- was levied on the parishioners for failure to repair the bridge. By July 1686 the bridge had been repaired by two contractors who charged £2, and Quarter Sessions ordered that the inhabitants should be estreated for £12.

It would almost seem that non-cooperation was contagious in the Washburn Valley about the middle of the seventeenth century. In July 1659 the parishes of Fewston and Weston were jointly indicted for the non repair of Dob Park Bridge. In the event the repair was carried out by the township of Clifton-with-Norwood whereupon several people in Fewston and Weston refused to pay their share until compelled to do so by Quarter Sessions. By 1738 the bridge was ruinous and irreparable, eventually being rebuilt at township expense, the cost being £50, towards which the Justices in Quarter Sessions granted £16 13s 4d.

Loyn Bridge

It was not always possible to determine exactly who was responsible for the repair and maintenance of a particular bridge. Floods in 1673 which swept away many of the bridges in Upper Wharfedale must also have taken place in the valleys west of Halifax where they wreaked havoc in the Ryburn Valley and seriously affected the bridge at Sowerby Bridge. It was subsequently examined and the damage assessed, although, because the water was so high it was impossible to gauge how much repair work would be needed. £150 or £200 was the figure given as the estimated cost of repair. Further probing on the part of the Justices revealed that, in fact, nothing had been allowed for repair of the 'said bridge for the space of fforty years last past.'[19] Furthermore there was no certain evidence as to who had built the bridge in the first place, nor who had been responsible for maintaining and repairing it. An order was therefore made that a Mr Hopkinson, an eminent local antiquary, should be asked to examine his records to see if he could ascertain who was responsible. On 16 July 1675 it was reported at Quarter Sessions in Leeds that Mr Hopkinson had examined his records and could find nothing whatsoever about Sowerby Bridge. The jury found, therefore, that the bridge should be repaired at the 'Charge of the whole Rideing' and £200 was estreated from the said Riding.[20]

Financial help from the Hundred, Wapentake or County towards the parishes for bridge repair was not new. It is probable that, as good men of the Hundred that there was an obligation on the holders of manors in Blackburnshire as early as the days of Edward the Confessor to repair their bridges. In 1684 the Justices in Quarter Sessions at Preston complied with an order from the Lord Chief Justice to give help in bridge building. This was that Loyn Bridge, near Hornby should be erected, the charge being shared by the whole county of Lancashire. The cost of the bridge was £1,250. The Justices were careful to say that this should not be a 'President to after time to make the Loyns Bridge a County Bridge nor to overthrow ancient agreement for each Hundred to repair and maintain their particular Bridges, the three County Bridges excepted.'[21]

It was shortly after this that the Justices became alarmed about the amount of money connected with bridge repair and the use, or misuse, of this money. In 1693 an Order was issued which stated that,

> This Court taking into consideration what great sums of money are estreated upon the country upon pretence of repair of Bridges, and how forward some persons are to demand and exact great sums for the repair of Bridges, whereas much smaller sums were sufficient, and the moneys raised have not been employed for the due repair of the Bridges, but converted to their own private uses, or disburst in extravagant expenses.[22]

Strong stuff.

These serious allegations resulted in the appointment of two people to investigate the misappropriation, if any, of public money. Much later examination of the evidence reveals that during the ten years in question (1683-93) £1,215 was spent on bridges, almost half on the three County bridges and the remainder on the twenty-seven Hundred bridges, working out at a little under £25 per bridge, which does not seem excessive.

By the middle of the seventeenth century the ford at Mitton was in a dangerous state and several lives had been lost while using it. In 1658 application was made for a bridge in order to make it safer for local inhabitants and also to provide a more convenient link between Blackburn and Slaidburn. As a 'border area' it was assumed that the West Riding would shoulder half of the cost. The Justices, many of whom were also the petitioners, agreed that a bridge should be built estimating the cost of Lancashire's half as £230. A letter was drafted to the West Riding Justices informing them of the facts and asking that they would bear the charges for the half of the bridge in their county. It was not until 1801 that a bridge was built to replace the ford ... by public subscription.

Private enterprise was responsible for some bridge building even as late as the seventeenth century; in the early part of that century Grassington Bridge was built by public subscription while Burnsall Bridge was built at the sole charge of Sir William Craven in 1609. Often the right of pontage was granted to the builders of a bridge to let them have the opportunity to recoup some of the money that had laid out initially.

Brockholes Bridge on the Preston to Blackburn highway was known as the Ha'penny Bridge because a ½d toll was formerly levied on all foot passengers crossing it. It was built in 1861 replacing a wooden one built in 1824.

In time, township bridges were raised to the status of Hundred or Wapentake bridges and subsequently the county assumed responsibility for them. Mytholmroyd Bridge, in the early seventeenth century a wooden bridge, had, by 1684 been rebuilt in stone; in 1752 it was a Wapentake bridge, chargeable on the wapentake of Agbrigg and Morley. Brearley Bridge, about a mile and a half downstream and now a graceful saddleback bridge, was raised from the status of a Wapentake bridge to a County Bridge about 1752. Ling Gill Bridge was repaired at the charge of the West Riding in 1765. By 1920 most of the wapentake bridges in the West Riding had been taken over by the County.

The County, like the smaller administrative authorities, was very anxious not to be liable for the expenditure of more money than was absolutely necessary and was at pains to establish exactly which bridges came under its administrative umbrella. In some counties Quarter Sessions required formal recognition of those bridges for which a particular county was responsible. As late as 1826 the JPs of Middlesex claimed only four bridges within the county as their responsibility, whereas by 1809 the JPs for Devonshire recognised 247 bridges. By 1702 the West Riding JPs assumed responsibility for 112 bridges, by 1752 the number had risen to 120. In the North Riding the number was less; in 1700 there were very few but by 1806 the number had risen to 115. A traveller observed that in no district in the kingdom of equal extent 'are the bridges, commonly called county bridges more numerous or better attended to' (than in the North Riding).[23] They were, for upwards of twenty years, under the care of John

Carr, the York Architect, and were generally marked with the initials Y.N.R.

Some counties formalised their bridge survey by producing a bridge book, a sort of Domesday Book of bridges. Such books were compiled in the West Riding in 1752 and in the North Riding in 1805. The administrative costs for 105 bridges were acknowledged by the West Riding and, by the North Riding for 100 while responsibility for others was divided with other counties having a common border, or with other administrative bodies. The West Riding shared the maintenance cost of some bridges with Westmorland, Derbyshire, the North Riding, York City and Tadcaster Town, and the North Riding shared with Westmorland, Durham, the West Riding, the East Riding and Richmond Corporation. In 1805 a *Book of Plans and Elevations of the Hundred Bridges in the Blackburn Hundred* was compiled, the number of bridges being seventy-two.

In Lancashire it was the practice to chisel on the parapet of the bridge its name and the fact that it was the responsibility of the county. This practice of chiselling is found in the West Riding too where a bridge was the joint responsibility of two townships; it can be found in Giggleswick and Settle where the bridge was at one time their joint responsibility, and also on Ferrybridge where the township of Brotherton as well as that of Ferrybridge shared expenses. Money for the maintenance of the bridges was normally acquired from local rates although in some cases where rebuilding rather than repair was necessary the Justices obtained special acts of parliament which gave them the right to levy tolls.

Written into the contract for bridge repair was the guarantee that the work would be well done ... 'the bridge to be built in an artfull, workmanlike and effectual manner' ... and 'John Law shall well and sufficiently erect and build the said new bridge.'[24]

It was usual for the JPs to appoint a supervisor or surveyor in order to check that the work was, in fact well done. In the beginning the supervisor would be a fellow JP but eventually the practice arose of appointing tradesmen and eventually one or more permanent surveyors was appointed at a small annual salary. In the West Riding two surveyors were paid small salaries from 1743; they were the men who made the survey of the county bridges in 1752. One of these surveyors was Robert Carr, a mason and quarry owner; many of the drawings were made by his son John Carr who succeeded him as one of the surveyors in 1761. In

1772 John Carr was appointed sole surveyor of bridges in the North Riding at an annual salary of £100, therefore he resigned his post with the West Riding.

The first salaried supervisor in the Blackburn Hundred was appointed in 1693, he was Mr Geoffrey Roby, steward to the Lady Hoghton. His special duty was the care of Ribble Bridge and Walton Cop and his annual salary was 40/- to be paid on every Michaelmas Day. In January 1717 the office of salaried bridgemaster was formally created with the appointment of two men to be supervisors of all the public hundred bridges in the hundred of Blackburn; the men being required 'from time to time view, take care of and repair all the said Bridges as shall be necessary.'[25] The Court of Quarter Sessions adroitly avoided the contentious issue of payment stating that 'for their services and salary the Court doth refer to the said Justices to set and settle the sum.' From that time forward, as far as Blackburn Hundred was concerned, there was a succession of salaried supervisors.

By the eighteenth century packhorse travel was dying out; wheeled carts were being increasingly used to transport goods. But in 1752 when the survey of bridges in the West Riding was made bridges were still very narrow, the great majority being between ten feet and fourteen feet wide. In Lancashire the position was no different, the width of Eadsford Bridge was eight feet, that of Whalley Bridge eight feet four inches and that of the bridge at Lower Hodder seven feet.

There is no wonder that bridges were so often in need of repair; the frequent pleas to Quarter Sessions in respect of some bridges, Ilkley Old Bridge is an example, were not due to shoddy workmanship as may be imagined. Passage of traffic over the bridges increased and by the late seventeenth and eighteenth centuries when carts were the usual mode of conveyance, bridges were still geared to packhorse dimensions, no wonder it was so often the parapets of the bridges which were damaged. One method of achieving greater security was to tie the coping-stones with iron clasps and sink them in lead. Stones which were displaced by the passage of traffic were recovered from the stream bed and set up again. The rate of payment for labourers working in 't' watter' was 10d rather than 8d a day.

Before man learnt to build durable and serviceable bridges he forded the stream or river at a shallow part, taking his carts and animals through. Stepping-stones were often used for foot passengers; in many places – Bolton Priory, Gargrave, Stainforth,

Selby Bridge

Hardcastle Crags – for instance, they remain, as a novelty rather than a necessity. But, in the absence of bridges stepping-stones remained in use until quite late in time. There were stepping, or, to use a local term, hypping-stones across the River Ribble where Brungerley Bridge was later built and there were hypping-stones across the River Darwen in 1695.

Near Buttocks farm on the Samlesbury and Hoghton boundary there was a ford and foot-bridge, the foot-bridge being washed away in 1830 and never reinstated; people crossed the river by means of stilts. In 1875 a man named Daniel Blake lived near the river. Having a sick cow he was in a great hurry to get to the vet and it was quicker for him to cross on stilts than walk all the way to Samlesbury Bridge. But there was only one lot of stilts so he carried the vet (who understandably was reluctant to agree to the arrangement) on his shoulders across the river on the return journey.

An alternative method of crossing rivers was by ferry-boat and the use of the ferries was common. There was a ferry service, served by two ferrymen in 1379 – which continued in regular use as the main means of communication between Samlesbury and Preston until 1826. The boatmen lived near the ferry on the Samlesbury side and in 1556 Hugh Welshman was ferryman but he paid such little attention to his work that he was fined 10/- and a special protest entered against him.

For about two hundred years the parishioners at Addingham were dependent on a ferry near West Hall. The bridge was swept away in the floods of 1673 and the bridge which replaced it suffered a similar fate fourteen years later. Repeated pleas to the magistrates for financial help fell on deaf ears and no bridge was built.

Ferries were used extensively on the River Ouse, in fact until the building of the bridge at Selby in 1792 the Yorkshire Ouse was crossed by only one bridge, the Ouse Bridge at York.

Near Wakefield there is an instance of a ferry in use at an even later date, that at Stanley crossed the River Calder at a point where a Roman Road once crossed the river. When the river had been made navigable it became too deep to ford and from the seventeenth century a ferry was used to make the crossing. In the early days it was small, too small to take a horse and cart so that these had to be taken separately. Pigs and pedestrians were charged 1d but sheep were taken for $\frac{1}{2}$d, horses were charged 2d and a horse and cart 6d. There was pressure for a bridge, pressure which, by the nineteenth century, became increasingly strong. It was not until 1879 that a bridge was built and it came about in a way which was not directly connected with traffic crossing the river.

The local Board of Health in Altofts was concerned with providing a water supply for the village, its great problem being getting pipes across the river. Negotiations were conducted with the Aire and Calder Navigation who, at first insisted that the pipes should be taken under the river, an expensive and possibly dangerous undertaking. The Board persisted, suggesting that it would be better to take the pipes over the river on a bridge, 'Could we not induce the Navigation to put up a bridge across which, for a consideration, our pipes might be laid and at the same time a great boon conferred on the public.'[26]

Eventually the Navigation undertook to make the bridge, the cost of which was £2,000 to which the Altofts Board had to contribute £400. The Lady of the Manor of Altofts, Mrs Meynell Ingram of Temple Newsam contributed a further £300.

The Navigation was empowered to charge ½d for pedestrians crossing the bridge and 2d for a horse, gelding, mare, ass or foal or wild beast not drawing. In 1895 special toll concessions were granted to miners going between Parkhill and Altofts granting a rate of 4½d weekly to men working full time and 3d for those working part time. Tolls were levied between 6 a.m. and 9 p.m. at which time the gates were locked for the night, this nightly locking continuing until 1956 when they had been broken into so frequently for 'emergency reasons' that they were not locked any more.

The tolls reflected the social change which had come to the area. When in December 1969 the bridge, which had become unsafe, was closed, motorised traffic was common. The tolls were 2d for a cycle, 3d for a motor cycle, and £4 4s for a yearly pass for a car. On 5 June 1971, a new bridge, free of toll, was opened.

To the modern mind, conditioned to items of expenditure totalling millions or even billions of pounds, the amounts of money bequeathed or assessed for the building and repair of bridges seem pitifully small. There is no satisfactory way of converting old values of money to modern ones; the best comparison is that of wages and prices. Even this has its drawbacks; for one thing the information is patchy and scanty. In the Middle Ages, and later, comparatively few people were sufficiently numerate to keep accounts – and to what end in any case? Some landlords, particularly rapacious or businesslike did compile rent rolls and in this respect the monastic houses were especially diligent. It is to them, therefore that we are indebted for much of the information which is available.

In the early Middle Ages manorial life was not geared to a cash economy, tenants paid their dues by working on the lord's land or by giving rent in kind. For some centuries this was superficially at any rate, a mutually agreeable arrangement, it provided the peasant with some sort of security and the lord was assured of an ever available, if somewhat unwilling labour force. The crops in the village were ready at the same time, as, under the common agricultural regime, all had been planted at the same time. And those of the lord had to be dealt with first. As time went on increasing discontent among the peasantry led the lords to commute rents and allow the tenants to pay in cash rather than by labour, or, in some cases, themselves to hire a substitute.

Occasionally in order to regularise this a schedule or extent was drawn up. This, broadly speaking, was a list of tenants with the work they were supposed to do for the lord of the manor and this was converted from service to a money rent. It was drawn up to determine the amount of money they were to pay in lieu of rent, not the money they were paid for working. But it does give some idea of the value of wage labour. A customary part of a man's daily work for his lord was, although by no means in every case, the provision by the lord of his midday meal.

Such a document is the Extent of the Manor of Monk Friston near Selby in Yorkshire, compiled in 1320. In it we read that a tenant who was to harrow one day at the spring seeding and another at the winter seeding and allowed each day one meal had his services valued, besides the meat, at 3d. Joining with a neighbour to cart hay for a day and having, between them presumably, two meals at the lord's charge, the work was valued, besides the meat, at 4d. Sheep washing and shearing, for an unspecified length of time, presumably a day, was valued at 1½d with 4d of beer. Carting wood for an unstated length of time, probably as long as it took, as he was required to cart four loads, was valued thus, 'he shall have meat once for his breakfast; which is worth besides the breakfast, 10d'. The extent goes on, 'Also he shall reap in harvest 14 days with one man, and he shall have every day one meal without drink; which work besides the meat is worth two shillings and fourpence.' Which seems to work out at about a penny or twopence a day.[27]

Wage rates varied from one part of the kingdom to another and there is no reason to suppose that as time progressed they rose. In Edward I's time (1272-1307) one penny was the average daily wage of a labourer whereas skilled workers such as masons or carpenters might have expected 3d or 4d.

In 1684 Loyn Bridge in Lancashire had cost the county the sum of £1,250. In 1673, in the Nelson district of Lancashire, a textile worker earned 4d a day with food and drink or 8d a day without food. Those who worked at home on materials 'put out' by a clothier got, in 1650 2s 2d for spinning a stone of wool, which was about a week's work.[28]

In 1745 10d was paid for setting watch on Sowerby Bridge, 4/6 was paid for three watch bills and 7d for two watch sticks. In 1723, in the Nelson district of Lancashire a weaver earned 3/6 for weaving a piece of cloth, which was about a week's work. Rather later in the century Arthur Young made a tour of the North of England in which he wrote about the improvements or lack of them in agriculture. He also listed the wages of people in some of the places he visited and in addition gave some of the prices. In Leeds weavers of broadcloths could earn as much as 10/6 a week all year if fully employed. However lack of employment meant that 8/- was the average wage. Weavers of other types of cloth earned on an average about 7/- per week. Wool combers earned between six and twelve shillings a week.[29]

He noted that there was much oatbread on sale at 1d for ten to eleven ounces while butter was 8d a pound, a pound being 18 or 19 ounces. Cheese, mutton, beef and pork were selling at 4d, for an unspecified amount, presumably a pound, while veal was $2\frac{1}{2}$d and bacon 7d.

At approximately the same period, in the Nelson district a skilled ploughman was paid 8d a day, a skilled man (an agricultural worker), received £5 10s a year and his food, and an apprentice in his last year 30/- with his keep. A dairymaid or housemaid received a shilling a week if she lived in but otherwise 2/- to 2/6. Journeymen craftsmen such as masons and joiners earned between 1s 6d and 1s 8d per day.[30]

So the bequeathing of half a mark (6/8), for the repair of a bridge would have been quite beyond the resources of the medieval peasant, it would have been equivalent to about eighty or forty days work. The amount spent on watch and ward and on the building of bridges was very large when compared with the wages of labour.

3   Tales of the Bridges

Changes made necessary by the complexities of twentieth-century living have affected bridges. Old structures, no longer capable of carrying heavy loads have been replaced; Ilkley Old Bridge and Ferrybridge for instance are now limited to pedestrian use. The Ilkley bridge spans the river in delicate and graceful style, and the later bridge is at sufficient distance not to crowd it and to enhance its dignity. Ferrybridge on the other hand, a finer bridge in many ways, is spoilt by the closeness of the new bridge over the Aire. Chantry Bridge, Wakefield, across which motor cars can still travel, has gained dignity since the cleaning and landscaping of the stonework and bank. At Otley the attractive medieval bridge has been spoilt architecturally by the (very

Ferrybridge

The Old Bridge, Ilkley

necessary) addition of a modern footbridge.

Perhaps the greatest benefit conferred by modern planning is that at Lancaster near what is arguably the finest bridge in the two counties, Skerton Bridge. The demolition of Green Ayre railway station, the removal of the track and the landscaping of the area by the river gives an uninterrupted view of the bridge.

Common to all the bridges are the subtleties of administration, but they have other links too. Wakefield and Rotherham have chapels upon them; those at Castleford, Ferrybridge, York, Skerton and Walton have been designed by architects, while two of the bridges are associated with the miraculous saving of lives. Three bridges are said to be the work of the Devil and others are famous for their association with well known historical events.

The bridge over Hebden Water, near Heptonstall and that over the River Calder near Sowerby were both very important for several reasons: as the former was near the manorial corn mill and the latter near a fulling mill, their existence was crucial to local life and trade. Their importance was still more far-reaching; trains of packhorses from places further north crossed Hebden Water to go from one side of the valley to the other and hence further south, whereas the bridge near Sowerby was on one of the main highways used by traffic from Newcastle, York, and Hull going to

Castleford Bridge

Manchester, Wigan, Liverpool and Cheshire, and in the reverse direction. It was Stirk Bridge, now demolished, which carried the packhorse route across the valley from Sowerby to Norland.

At the time of the Industrial Revolution the hill settlements of Heptonstall and Sowerby gradually became less important and the new towns which grew round the bridges, Hebden Bridge and Sowerby Bridge, became important centres of industry. The old bridge over the Hebden Water has remained virtually unchanged and it is across another bridge further downstream that the traffic thunders up and down the valley, leaving the packhorse bridge to pedestrians and duckfeeders. A wide bridge upstream from the old bridge carries some traffic into the town particularly on market days. Lower down the valley however, on the River Calder, the bridge near Sowerby, Sowerby Bridge, now has painted metal parapets and carries a wide metalled road. Underneath this 'Industrial Revolution' cladding can be seen the arches of the old bridge.

It is likely that there was a bridge over the River Calder at this point in early days and that the east-west route has been an important one for centuries. In the early sixteenth century several bequests are recorded towards the making of a stone bridge there, among them there was one from a man named Wm. Holleroode (Holroyd), quite a usual local surname. This stone bridge was built from money which was supplied by the men who used it.

The packhorse bridge in Bingley which carried the main traffic through the town was not built from stone until 1723 and the two bridges which now carry the main roads into the town were not built in stone until relatively late in time. Bingley Bridge was, until towards the end of the seventeenth century a narrow wooden bridge. In 1685 it was built in stone and in 1775 was repaired and widened. It is known locally as Ireland Bridge, the name originally having a facetious meaning. As the river at this point separated two manors and ownerships, crossing it was compared with crossing the channel between England and Ireland. The bridge at the other end of the town, Cottingley Bridge, was widened a year or two after Ireland Bridge and there was great difficulty in getting sufficiently firm foundations for the piers because of the great thickness of loose gravel. The contractor for the bridge was Barnabas Morvill who, in 1770 was one of the contractors for the mason work at the Three Rise and Five Rise locks on the Leeds and Liverpool Canal. He was very much out of pocket with the Cottingley Bridge contract, and in an attempt to put this right he put his case to the West Riding Justices at Pontefract on 3 April 1780. It was ordered that a gratuity of £40 be given to Mr Morvill because he had suffered extraordinary expense in the proper execution of the work.

Sowerby Bridge, an important crossing point for traffic between Yorkshire and Lancashire was watched at various times of crisis. Other bridges where watch was important were Wensley and Kilgram in Wensleydale which were watched day and night during the terrible cattle plague in the middle of the eighteenth century. In July 1749 £7 17s 6d was spent for watching Wensley Bridge. For watching Kilgram Bridge, from 19 December 1748 to 4 February following, the sum of £8 10s was paid by order of the Justices sitting in Northallerton in July 1749, and similar amounts were also sanctioned for watching other Richmondshire bridges. The rate of pay was 10d per man during daylight hours and 1/8 per two men during the hours of darkness, which amounts to the same thing. The employment of two men together, at night, would no doubt be a precaution, not infallible, that one of them would remain awake. The plague seems to have broken out, or to

Kilgram Bridge

have been recognised, by the local authorities, in the Spring of 1747 and it was not until 12 July 1753 that the Justices felt that it was sufficiently safe to allow fairs to open.

This virulent cattle plague which raged for six years throughout much of England resulted in great losses to farmers who were required to slaughter their herds. Fairs and markets were suspended – as of course the word fair had a different meaning then from now; fairs in the eighteenth century were held principally for the trading of animals. Warning boards were erected on the highways in the infected districts.

Leland said of Wensley Bridge – 'a great Bridge of stone was made many yers sins by a good person of Wencelaw called Alwine' ... It was in fact originally built at the expense of Revd John Alwent, a rector of Wensley who died in 1430. In 1400 the sum of £40 was left for its upkeep by Richard, Lord Scrope of Bolton. In 1586 it was repaired at a cost of £60 and subsequent repairs have taken place, the bridge being widened in the early nineteenth century.

It is highly likely that Richmond Bridge was also watched during the cattle plague of the eighteenth century, but long before this terrible scourge Leland described the bridge at Richmond as having four arches on the centre of which stood a small building where a watchman was stationed to alarm the town in times of danger. Tolls for the upkeep of the bridge were imposed on corn and cattle which passed over it. In 1622 these were let at 44/- a year. In 1739 the maintenance of the bridge was vested in the hands of a number of Justices of the Peace who were empowered to contract with workmen for its repair. In 1771 the bridge was much damaged by flood and in 1789 was replaced by another stone structure.

Kilgram Bridge has a claim to notoriety other than that associated with the cattle plague; it is reputed to be of very old foundation and to be linked with the Devil. Of Kilgram Bridge it is said,

> Of Kilgram Bridge we now did talk
> And I had answer given
> That here a bridge was of stone work
> In hundred years eleven.[1]

The bridge is supposed to have been built by Norman architects between the completion of Richmond Castle in 1070 and the building of Jervaulx Abbey in 1145. Either that or his Satanic Majesty was responsible. The legend, and this legendary tale is told of other bridges in the North of England, is that at this point the river was excessively turbulent and although the people of the district built bridge after bridge, each was swept away by the swiftly flowing, uncontrollable waters of the river. Eventually the Devil took a hand, making a handsome offer to the people of Kilgram. He offered to build a bridge which would be indestructible, but attached a condition. This was that in return for the bridge the inhabitants should sacrifice to him the first living creature to cross it. The terms were agreed and the bridge was built, the Devil no doubt sitting back to await his prize. A shepherd of the vicinity who had his wits about him, was the first to cross. He defeated the intentions of the Evil One by swimming across the river and, on reaching the other side, whistled for his dog which came across the bridge. The Devil's spoil was therefore a dog whose name was Grim, hence the name of the bridge, Kill Grim.

The bridge is one stone short: another version of the Satanic story being that some dreadful fate˙ would befall the luckless inhabitants of Kilgram should the bridge ever be finished. An alternative explanation offered was that because of the missing stone the ultimate collapse of the bridge would be hastened in which case his Satanic majesty would gain handsome profit from stealing the goods of whoever happened to be on the bridge when it collapsed.

Kilgram Bridge has been kept in a good state of repair, in 1585 a hundred a marks were spent on it. In 1611 it again needed repair and the Justices ordered that, 'if the inhabitants nigh to the same will disburse so much as will sufficiently repair the same, the Justices shall, upon receiving a just accompt of such disbursements, take order that a rate shall be made to levie such somme of money of the County with the convenient spede that may be, as shall be reasonably disbursed about the same.'[2] Care has always been taken never to replace the missing stone.

Hell Gill Bridge, on the border of the old counties of Yorkshire and Westmorland is another associated with the Devil. Legend asserts that when the Devil built the first bridge the straps of his apron, in which he carried the stones he needed, broke as he was flying from a mountain top. The apron and its contents fell into the River Eden with such force that Kail Pot was created. Another legend tells us that Dick Turpin was once waylaid by the constables of Westmorland at Devil's Bridge, but, urged by the spur and a slight tug on the rein Black Bess leapt over the abyss into the county of Yorkshire where the warrant could not be served.

Yet another legend tells of the foundation of a bridge near Grassington. In North Yorkshire the River Dibb flows in a valley between Pateley Bridge and Grassington. At the time when Fountains Abbey was in its heyday a shoemaker who was a tenant of the abbey lived at Thorp sub Montem and twice each year he travelled along the road in order to pay his rent to the Abbot, return the shoes he had repaired and collect another consignment. Usually his journey was uneventful but on one occasion he had a nightmare during the night before he was due to travel; the scene in the nightmare was vivid, depicting a wild and rocky ravine in which he struggled with the Devil. However he didn't let this deter him and set forth as usual on his journey, transacted his business with the monastery and began his return trip. To his dismay he found that the small stream which he usually crossed with ease had swollen to a great and roaring torrent and it was with some difficulty and not a little danger that he managed to struggle through the raging waters. Tired, but relieved that he was safely on the other side he sat down to dry his things and, in order to cheer himself up sang a little ditty the chorus of which ran, 'Sing luck a down, heigh down, ho down derry.' At the end he was startled to hear another voice join in, adding the words, 'Tol lol derol, darel dol, dolde derry.' He was even more startled when the owner of the voice revealed himself as Satan.

To his surprise Satan asked if there was anything he could do to help whereupon the shoemaker replied that a bridge should be built across the stream at that point. Satan told him to return in four days when he would receive a great surprise. The news of his meeting with Satan and the promise spread round the village and when the shoemaker, on the fourth day, accompanied by thirty or forty villagers, returned to the place it was to find a beautiful and substantial bridge there.

The parish priest was among the crowd; he sprinkled the bridge with holy water, ordered that a cross should be placed at each approach to it and then said it was safe for all Christian people to use. It remained like this until the puritan minister of Pateley Bridge at the time of the Commonwealth, thinking that the story was tainted with popery, caused the crosses to be removed on the grounds that they were idolatrous. In time the bridge fell into disuse and later another was built to replace it. But the name remained; it is still called the Devil's Bridge.

Not all stories concerned with bridges deal with the work of the Devil. A beggar, named Thomas Ferrers[3] was crossing the river at Egton in North Yorkshire, by means of stepping stones, at this time the only way of crossing. As the river was in flood it was a difficult, not to say dangerous, venture. He fell in and was almost drowned before he managed to struggle out. Safely on dry land he made a vow that if ever he should have the means to do so he would build a bridge at that spot for the convenience of travellers. Eventually he went to Hull, where, in the course of time he made his fortune. He did not forget his vow and, eventually, built a bridge on which are his initials and the date 1621. This is claimed to be the origin of the name Beggar's Bridge.

An alternative version of the story claims the title Lovers

Ouse Bridge, York

Bridge. In this version the man who was trying to cross was going to visit his lady love, and he too was almost submerged, but, after struggling out did not again attempt to cross. He went away to seek his fortune vowing that he would return, a wealthy man, and claim the hand of his bride and also build a bridge; which two ambitions he eventually realised.

The most charming of the bridge legends concerns Wharfedale. Near the village of Linton-in-Craven is a very attractive fourteenth century bridge known as Li'le Emily's Bridge, or Emily Norton's Bridge.

The lineage of the family is associated with Norton Conyers, John Coigniers (otherwise Norton) married Anne, the daughter and heiress of William of Rylstone and therefore inherited the Rylstone estate. The Nortons were staunch Roman Catholics and in 1536 joined the rebellion, the Pilgrimage of Grace led by Robert Aske in defence of the Roman Catholic religion. In 1569 there was another rebellion, the Rising of the North, in the interests of the Catholic Mary Stuart. Prominent in this rebellion was the Norton family, eight of whose members were eager to join. Francis, the eldest son, however, saw nothing but disaster for the family from this course of action and tried to dissuade his father from joining. The rebellion was a disaster and, as a consequence, the estates of the Nortons were confiscated and came into the hands of the Cliffords. Francis Norton escaped retribution for a time but was eventually captured and killed, legend has it on Barden Fell. He was buried at Bolton Priory and it was to his grave that his sister Emily came. She was accompanied in her weekly pilgrimage by a white doe which had been captured by Francis and given to her. After her death the doe was to be seen wandering in the ruins of Bolton Priory. The legend has been immortalised by Wordsworth. The Nortons also owned much of Threshfield village and it was said that during the rebellion Emily lived there, walking to church across the bridge which has been named after her.

The story, delightful and whimsical though it is, is just that, a piece of fiction. Francis's death on Barden Fell is based on legend. It would have been odd for Emily, a staunch Catholic in hiding, to be a regular attender at the Protestant church in Linton. In fact, there never was a woman called Emily; it was a name never used in the family.

A legend about Ouse Bridge in York has also been claimed by

Pontefract and Ferrybridge. In the case of Pontefract, charters and other documents designated it *Pons Fractus* many years before the story of York. When William, lately restored to his Archbishopric, arrived at York in 1154 he was met by a large and enthusiastic crowd of people. As they were going over Ouse Bridge, which in those days was a wooden structure, the weight and turbulence of the crowd was so great that the fastenings at the end of the bridge broke; the whole structure gave way and the crowd was flung into the river. When the Archbishop saw the drowning throng he made the sign of the Cross over them and

Brungerley Bridge

prayed to God that they would be saved. No sooner was the prayer uttered than the surging waters themselves became a bridge and all the people were able to get to terra firma with nobody being hurt. On the repaired bridge a chapel was built in memory of this miracle. The chapel, dedicated to St William was only taken down when the bridge was rebuilt centuries later.

Other bridges or river crossings were scenes of fact rather than fiction. One such place is the present Brungerley Bridge. After the heavy and bloody defeat of the Lancastrians at the Battle of Towton in the Wars of the Roses it is probable that Henry VI and his Queen, Margaret, fled through Newcastle to Berwick. Rumour said that he eventually took refuge in Wales but it is more than likely that he never left Scotland. In the Spring of 1464 the North rose in favour of Henry and he joined the rebels but unfortunately for him the uprising was crushed at the battles of Hedgley Moor and Hexham and Henry narrowly avoided capture. In June of that year the Scots concluded a truce with the Yorkists and abandoned Henry's cause although the gentry and peasantry of the North remained faithful to him. He hid in disguise in various parts of the north of England; it was reported that at one time he took refuge in a monastery and was more than once entertained at Crackenthorpe near Appleby. His favourite refuge was, however in Upper Ribblesdale and it was while he was sitting at dinner at Waddington Hall that he was recognised. He escaped but was captured near the hypping-stones (at the site of the present Brungerley Bridge) by Thomas Talbot of Bashall and his cousin John. A wooden bridge was built at this place at some later date and this was washed away in 1814 since which time the stone bridge was built.

It is likely that a bridge, probably a wooden one upon stone piers, existed on the site of the ancient bridge at Lower Hodder at an early date, as in 1329 Adam Walton, the Rector of Mitton had testified that the Bridge over the Hodder was frequently broken down, the river being subject to floods. In 1563 the 'sufficient and abyll bryge of stone'[4] was built by Roger Crossley at Lower Hodder and it is no doubt this which is reputed to be that used by Oliver Cromwell and his army on August 16th 1648, the day before the Battle of Ribbleton Moor at Preston. The fact that he did cross the Hodder is quite true but it is not certain whether it was by this bridge or another, which has been demolished, which at one time stood near the present Hodder Bridge.

Stamford Bridge

Apart from its connection with football the name Stamford Bridge is associated by most people with the Norman Conquest. There were three contenders for the throne which became vacant on the demise of Edward the Confessor in 1066, Harald Hardrada of Norway, Harold of Wessex, and William, Duke of Normandy. It was Harold of Wessex who was designated as successor and who was crowned on January 6th 1066.

His rivals were swift to mobilise their forces; Harald of Norway, aided and abetted by Harold's brother Tostig, was the first to invade. In September 1066 his fleet sailed up the Humber, defeated the army of Earl Edwin and Earl Morcar in the battle at Fulford and encamped near Stamford Bridge. Harold, collecting an army en route, marched via the Roman roads from London, and reached Stamford Bridge within five days of the defeat of Edwin and Morcar. The same day he confronted the Norwegians. Harald was mortally wounded by an arrow in his throat and Tostig assumed command. Harold offered his brother peace, an offer which was declined; the Norwegian army stating that they would rather die than accept peace from an Englishman. Harold's victory was decisive, and whereas it had taken three hundred ships to bring the Norwegians to England, twenty-five ships sufficed to take the survivors back again.

According to local legend the fiercest part of the fight was when the two armies struggled to gain control of the bridge itself. A

Norwegian, of immense stature and very great strength positioned himself on the end of the bridge and kept the English at bay slaying them in great numbers, so much so that soon he had a ring of corpses at his feet. Eventually one of the English soldiers set forth on the river in a washing tub, paddled his craft to a position where he was right under the bridge and stabbed the Norwegian through the open timbers. This feat, so it is said, is commemorated every year by the people of Stamford Bridge. They make a huge pie in the shape of a wash tub and this is shared among the villagers.

The bridge, in the illustration of the BBC Hulton Picture Library, shows a double-arched, stone, packhorse type bridge; but it is more likely that the bridge of 1066 was made of wood. Later another wooden bridge was built which was removed in 1727 when it fell into decay. The present bridge was built, at the charge of the County, about a hundred yards below the old one.

Until about the middle of the eighteenth century there was only one bridge over the River Ribble which gave direct communication with Preston; that at Walton: on the south-west side of the town the river was crossed by a ferry and two fords. In 1400, letters patent were granted for pontage on a bridge near the town of Preston. The order said that because of the great overflowing of the water and the inroads made by the floating masses of ice and frost, the existing bridge had become so much broken and partially destroyed that it was unsafe for travellers to cross it. It was proposed therefore, to erect a stone bridge near to the old one, and the right to charge certain tolls for the next three years was granted. The tolls were, horses, oxen, cows, $\frac{1}{4}$d; hides of all kinds, fresh or tanned, $\frac{1}{4}$d; ten sheep or pigs, $\frac{1}{2}$d; a horse load of cloth, $\frac{1}{2}$d; a hogshead of wine, 1d; trusses of cloth carried in a coil, 1d; 1,000 herrings, $\frac{1}{2}$d; a horse load of sea fish, $\frac{1}{2}$d; 100 planks, $\frac{1}{2}$d; millstones, $\frac{1}{2}$d; 1,000 faggots, $\frac{1}{2}$d; a quarter of salt, $\frac{1}{4}$d; a quarter weight of cheese or butter, $\frac{1}{2}$d; iron, pewter, copper, lead and wool all paid toll of similar amounts.[5]

Seven years later the stone bridge had still not been built and representations were made that the danger to passengers was now greater than ever. The great expense of carrying out the work had prevented its being done. (To 1980s ears the words sound dismally familiar.) In response to this appeal the right to charge toll for a further three years was granted. Among the articles on which toll could be charged were – Irish cloth (Galway) and

Old Penwortham Bridge

worsted; honey; pairs of wheels; treetrunks; coal; small vessels or boats coming to the bridge; river boats laden with mussels, crops of reeds and the like.

Leland mentions the great stone bridge of Rybill having five great arches and it was this bridge – also alluded to as Bridge of Ribble by Cromwell in his dispatch as having been taken at 'push of pike' after stubborn resistance by the enemy. This bridge was for a long time regarded as an important factor in military strategy.

The present bridge, standing a little distance above that of Leland is a graceful structure consisting of three large arches. On the north side is a stone bearing the inscription 'Built by John Saml and Robt Laws in 1799, 80 and 81 under the Inspection of Richd Threlfall. Cost £4,200.

In 1750 an Act of Parliament was obtained giving permission to build a bridge across the Ribble between Penwortham and Preston. This, opened in 1755 was financed by public subscription; the Corporation, Members of Parliament for Preston and gentlemen who owned property in the area being the main contributors.

About a year after its opening the bridge collapsed, one of the central piers gave way and shortly afterwards five of the arches collapsed. A replacement for this needed a new Act of Parliament, an act which sanctioned the provision of £2,000 from the County for the purposes of reconstruction. Subsequent maintenance was to be secured by means of tolls. The bridge was re-erected in 1759. A more modern bridge was built in the twentieth century.

Bridges other than those in the immediate vicinity of Preston crossed the Ribble. Ribchester Bridge, which is a fine structure, is the only road crossing of the Ribble for about eighteen miles, as the river flows. Mitton is the next crossing upstream and Preston downstream. There is considerable doubt as to the antiquity of a bridge over the Ribble at Ribchester. In Roman times there was an important ford. In 1669 the old bridge between Clayton-le-Dale and Ribchester was replaced by another bridge which was eventually washed down by a flood. In 1769 tenders were invited for the rebuilding of the County bridge called Ribchester Bridge. In 1774 the present bridge was built.

A bridge over the Ribble which bordered the administrative area of the West Riding was that at Paythorne which is recorded in the West Riding *Book of Bridges* of 1752. Part of this bridge at any rate seems to have been of considerable age as two of the arches have a ribbed understructure. The other part of the bridge is of a later date and is of rough stone.

There was a bridge from early times at Eadsford near Clitheroe and it was, until the seventeenth century, the only bridge spanning the Ribble above Preston. It was known therefore, as the Bridge of Ribble. This bridge in 1339, was seriously damaged by various floods and therefore Royal Letters Patent were obtained to legalise the taking of tolls for a period of two years in aid of its repair. As it was the only bridge for many miles much traffic would have to use it in order to go north and east and likewise traffic coming in the reverse direction. The bridge was rebuilt in the 18th century.

The list of tolls is long and varied, much more so than that for Walton Bridge in 1400. Some of the terms used are now obsolete; frail and fardle for instance. Medieval measure and weight were locally determined and therefore differed from area to area, a fardle (fardel) was a bundle, a little pack, a parcel, and as such would no doubt have varied in size. A frail was a rush basket which was used for packing figs, raisins etc. The term was also used to describe the quantity of dried fruit the container held and

	d.
, barley, beans, and peas (if for sale), for every arter	1
, the quarter	¼
ings, the 1000 or last	½
fish, the cart-load	4
the horse-load	1
l, the sack	2
the poise	½
se, mare, ox, or cow, each	½
of horse, mare, ox, or cow, fresh and salted or nned	¼
hides, the last	1
p or swine, for ten	1
ase, tallow, butter, and cheese, by the poise	¼
per, the hundred-weight	2
onds, the hundred-weight	1
ain, the hundred-weight	½
s, the frail	¼
sins, the frail	¼
lick, the bunch	¼
ons, the bunch	¼
e, the cask	2
ad, the quarter	1
x, the hundred-weight	2
sels, the thousand	¼
ware, the cwt.	2
hs, bound up, the fardle, of the value of 24*s.* r more	1
d, the carrat	2
ry fardle not bound	¼
and ale, the cask	1
ch of bacon	¼

	d.
Alum, the cwt.	2
Salt, the quarter	½
Linen web of canvas, the cwt.	1
Each whole cloth	½
Fleeces of sheep, the cwt.	2
Skins of lambs, rabbits, and hares, the cwt.	½
Steel, the sheaf	¼
Grindstones, each	½
Honey, the horse load	1
,, the cask	3
For every fardle of merchandise of any kind, exceeding the value of two shillings	¼
Goats, for ten	1
For every fresh salmon	¼
For every lamprey before Easter	¼
For ten fleeces	½
Cloths of Galway, Man, Ireland, and Worsted, the 100, of	1
Tan, the horseload	½
Avoir du poise, the cwt.	1
Copper, the cwt.	½
Flour, the quarter	1
Cordewayn (Cordova shoe-leather) the bale	3
Roof nails, the 1000	¼
Iron nails, for horseshoes and carts, the cwt.	½
Nails of all sorts, except for carts and roofing, 2000	¼
Every caldron and lead for brewing	¼
Every horseload, for sale	¼
Hemp, the horseload	¼
Every carcase of bull and cow	¼
Anything for sale, not yet specified, exceeding the value of five shillings	¼

A carrat of lead is shown to have been 150 stone by the following passage of the Compotus of Simon Noel, eiver of Clitheroe, 1306. Et xiij li. xiij s. iij d. in ix. carratis et dimidio, septem pedibus, et j petra plumbo emptis e de eisdem (*i.e.* operantibus), unde vj. petre faciunt pedem, et xxv. pedes faciunt carratam.

Tolls at Eadsford Bridge in 1339[6]

this too varied, being anything between thirty to seventy-five pounds. The word poise is here the most interesting, meaning the amount that a thing weighs, while avoir du poise means, in the context in which it was used on this list, merchandise sold by weight, a meaning which is now obsolete. A quarter was a dry measure used for grain and was eight bushels, but even the bushel varied in capacity from place to place while the hundredweight varied locally from anything between a hundred and hundred and twenty pounds. A last was a load varying in weight with the type of merchandise carried and which also varied from locality to locality. A carat of lead was 150 stones. A sheaf is a bundle of things bound side by side, presumably steel rods.

It was evidently the practice to levy the toll in accordance with the scarcity value of the commodity, the rarer items having a high toll whereas the commoner commodities were given a lower toll. The toll charged on oats, for instance, the grain staple of the northern peasantry, was a quarter of that on the other grains and pulses, including peas and beans, which is surprising. It was also, which is not at all surprising, a quarter of the toll on flour. Large animals were charged $\frac{1}{2}$d each, whereas sheep, pigs and goats were ten a penny.

The more exotic products such as Cordovan leather carried a high toll, also pepper and wine. What is surprising is the carriage of such large quantities of pepper, almonds and cumin. Sea fish and honey were valuable items – a horseload of sea fish only paid $\frac{1}{2}$d at Walton in 1400, but then Walton is nearer the sea than Eadsford Bridge. Teasels in such large quantities and woad point to the existence of a textile industry, while alum would probably have been used in the manufacture of dyes and also in tanning leather.

To the modern mind the toll of only $\frac{1}{4}$d on fresh salmon seems very small but in earlier days and in the Ribble itself salmon were quite common, for the more well-to-do of course.

And as if the list were not long enough, any omissions were covered by the blanket expressions 'for every fardle of merchandise of any kind, exceeding the value of two shillings,' and 'Anything for sale, not yet specified, exceeding the value of five shillings.'

Salt, at only a halfpenny, was a surprisingly small toll as salt was one of the most important commodities in the medieval economy, being used to preserve meat. The slaughter of a large number of animals took place at Michaelmas as there was insufficient food to keep them alive during the winter months. Meat was preserved by drying or salting, and salt was also used to preserve fish.

One end of this bridge stood within the township of Clitheroe and in 1657 the Borough claimed the right, which was one held by

Whalley Bridge

all other boroughs in the County, to be free of all dues and taxes which were levied towards the building of bridges. The borough evidently wanted no financial responsibility for its own bridge. The Corporation was successful in its plea for exemption even to the extent of being refunded money which had already been paid. In 1634 23/4 was deducted, in favour of Clitheroe, for the repair of Whalley and Fenisford Bridges, while in 1657 the Justices not only agreed to Clitheroe being 'freed from being taxed towards the repair of any public bridges except those within (the borough), but 'that the moneys paid towards the repair of Ribble Bridge shall be repaid by the overseers thereof.'⁷ If, as was likely, there *was* no money in hand, cash was to be taken from the next assessment. This single exemption within Blackburn Hundred was a source of annoyance and irritation to other townships and attempts were made unsuccessfully, to get the order reversed.

Another fine bridge is the road bridge over the River Calder at Whalley. It is a substantial structure which appears to be modern and is very pleasing. On both the upstream and the downstream sides the parapet contains two resting-places for travellers, semicircular rather than triangular. The bridge has three segmental arches each with a prominent surround; near the springs of the arches the stones are indented while in the middle, over the crown of the arch the stones have straight edges. On each arch surround there is a mounting of stone so that the arches look even more solid. Also giving an increased impression of solidity are the piers which come from the water right to the top of the parapet, forming the semicircular resting places. The fact that

Paythorne Bridge

they are rusticated again adds to the solid substantial appearance of the bridge. When however one goes beneath the bridge one can see that it is of ancient foundation. Two of the arches have a ribbed understructure and the bridge has been widened twice, both on the upstream and the downstream side. The ribbed understructure is not uncommon in the bridges of the two counties, being apparent, to name a few instances, at Paythorne, Kildwick, Otley, Wakefield and Giggleswick.

Tradition invested the great bridge over the Lune at Lancaster with a picturesque story, proving the existence of a bridge in Danish times – on the demolition of a later bridge a pot was found containing several brass coins dating from the time of King Canute. Certainly a bridge did exist on this site before the thirteenth century but the first reference to it for which there is documentary backing is that of 1215 when King John instructed that the Abbot and monks of Furness should be granted timber from the forest of Lancaster for the repair of their fishery at the bridge.

This bridge was of wood, in 1251-52 Geoffrey de Langley (Chief Justice of the Forest north of the Trent) was instructed to supply thirty oak trees for its repair; in 1373 six score oak trees were used for its repair. Doubtless the elements were in part responsible for the decay of the bridge but considerable damage was caused by excessively heavy loads being taken over it. Not all goods of course *were* taken over the bridge, because, as elsewhere a means had been found of cheating the system and avoiding pontage by using a boat to convey goods across the river. So, the authorities, anxious to be one jump ahead of the swindlers, re-established their control by, in 1379, securing permission to apply pontage to goods taken over the River Lune for a distance of approximately three miles on either side of the bridge.

By 1590 the condition of the bridge was bad, and had again deteriorated during the next half century. In 1654 carpenters were asked to assist in its repair. It seems that at that comparatively late date it was still a wooden bridge. In 1684 when more major repairs were carried out timber was used.

By 1715 the Scottish rebels were approaching Lancaster and a suggestion was made that the bridge should be demolished to halt their progress. Part of it had already been demolished when it was pointed out that the river was, at low water, fordable further down. Work on demolition was stopped.

Skerton Bridge, Lancaster

By 1770 the Corporation were interested in the possibility of a new bridge but it was not until 1782 that a petition was presented to the House of Commons about the matter of taking down the old bridge and building a new one. The Petition lay on the table for some time, during which the condition of the old bridge was deteriorating. In 1797 the gap in the parapet wall made at the time of the 1715 rebellion was apparent; by 1800 all the parapet walls had been destroyed. There were serious accidents: in 1795 one of the wheels came off a cart – the cart, the horse, and woman in charge all fell over the side of the bridge through a gap in the parapet wall; later that year there was a similar accident. In 1789 a man was killed and in 1801 a six-year-old boy injured by falling through the parapet wall.

By 1787 the new bridge, Skerton Bridge, was completed. The old bridge was not closed until 1802 and the arch on the Skerton side pulled down. Prizes had been offered of twenty, ten and five guineas for the best design for a new bridge and the first prize went to Thomas Harrison of Chester, who, because of his rather shy nature and unworldly temperament and his relative isolation away from London and the hub of affairs, was not well known. He combined the functions of architect and engineer with skill, and Skerton Bridge which cost £14,000 is an impressive and significant structure. It has five elliptical arches divided by niches, each intended to take a statue, and an impressive balustrade. It was linked in Lancaster to an improved residential and road scheme and as such was a significant piece of town planning.

It was the first of a magnificent series of bridges and an aqueduct all of which were designed by Harrison's friend John Rennie – London Bridge, Waterloo Bridge, Kelso Bridge and the Lune Aqueduct. It was, when built, the first large-scale masonry bridge in this country with a level road surface from bank to bank.

The Lune, near Caton, was crossed by a ford until, as a result of funds subscribed by some of the resident gentry of the district a bridge was built in 1805 a little lower down from the ford. This had three elliptical arches of stone, two having a sixty-five-foot span and one a sixty-three-foot span. The height of the roadway above low water was about thirty-nine feet and the width between parapets was sixteen feet. This, known as the 'penny bridge' as a penny was charged to cross it, was faulty in design, nor was the workmanship of very good standard.

By 1880 the fabric had become unsafe for traffic, about a third of the arch stones being cracked. The County was asked to take over the bridge and eventually they agreed and also decided that £1,000 be paid to the proprietors by way of compensation.

A new bridge was considered and the County Surveyor estimated that this would cost £11,000. Some members of the committee contended that this was excessively high and thought a plain substantial bridge could be obtained for less money. The matter was thrown open to competition and eventually the design of the County Surveyor was accepted. The matter was put out to tender and that of Benton and Woodiwiss of Derby for £8,500 was accepted. The work was to be completed by 31 January 1884.

There were problems; it was difficult to secure stable foundations in the bed of the Lune; and, because of the liability of the river to flood the erection of scaffolding of sufficient strength to carry the weight of the equipment was a problem. However by 29 January 1883 the ceremony of placing the keystone of the last arch of the bridge was performed by Miss Grey of Escowbank in the presence of several of the gentry of the neighbourhood.

Lune aqueduct

The bridge was built of stone from quarries in Horsforth and Pool Bank near Leeds. The opening ceremony, in good weather, was performed by Mr. H. Garnett, chairman of the Court of Quarter Sessions. He was accompanied by the contractors, the architect and several local gentry and clergy and members of the public. He congratulated the contractors on completing the work ahead of time.

There are two bridge chapels still in Yorkshire, one at Wakefield, the other at Rotherham. In common with many other places Wakefield had a wooden bridge in the early days. In 1308 there was severe flooding causing great damage to this wooden structure which spanned the River Calder at the bottom of Kirkgate. Repairs were carried out but twenty-two years later there was a prolonged spell of heavy rain which lasted from Christmas Eve until the Thursday before Lent. The river rose so rapidly and to such a great extent that all work was stopped at the corn and fulling mills. The bridge was again damaged, this time so badly that townsmen realised that a new one was necessary.

It was decided that it should be built of stone and application was made for a charter giving permission for this to be built. In 1342 Edward III granted to the bailiffs of Wakefield the tolls for three years on all goods for sale and animals passing over the bridge 'as a help towards the repairs and improvements of the said bridge'.[8] This bridge over the River Calder consisted of nine arches, the eastern side with its four-pointed ribbed arches, was built in 1342, the width at that time being about sixteen feet between parapets.

There is some difference of opinion about when the chapel was built, one authority puts it at 1342, at the same time as the rebuilding of the bridge. Another suggestion is that it was built in 1362, the occasion being the progress of Edward III throughout the country to commemorate his having completed his fiftieth year. Another body of opinion favours 1460 as the date of the building of the chapel. It is probable that it was built in the reign of Edward III and re-endowed in the reign of Edward IV. Its cresset light acted as a guide to the wayfarer and the navigator on the Calder. It was also visited by travellers who wished to give thanks in a chapel dedicated to the Virgin for their preservation from danger by 'flood and field', a quaint and archaic expression, perhaps meaning preservation from being killed in the field of battle.

Wakefield Bridge

It seems to have been served in early days by two priests who had a house close by. At the time of the compilation of the 'Valor Ecclesiasticus' in 1534, the yearly value of the chapel was £12 8 11d and the two priests, Richard Saul and Tristram Harton had each an income of £6 3 7d. When the Dissolution came the value was £14 15 3d; the ornaments and vestments were valued at £1 2 6d and the plate at £4 4 8d. The two priests were described as 'unlearned' and in 1548 were pensioned off with £5 per year each, so long as nothing better in the way of preferment came their way. The chantry was spared, 'for that it is builded upon the myddlemoste arche of the said bridge of Wakefield being no smalle strengthe therunto'[9] and service was resumed in the chapel when the Catholic Queen Mary came to the throne. At her death the priests were again driven out and the chapel and its land given over to the trustees of the poor who let the property off to tenants.

The building had a varied career; at one time it was the premises of a dealer in old clothes and was later converted to the use of a warehouseman, after which it was used as a library and news room. Some time later it was used by a maker of cheesecakes, then by a corn factor and later still it was the premises of a tailor. In 1842 a movement for its restoration as a chapel was started. The architect G.G. Scott took down the whole of the chantry above the basement and rebuilt it on the exact lines of the previous building.

A modern bridge now carries the very considerable and heavy traffic across the Calder. The chantry bridge remains, used mainly by pedestrians and also by some vehicular traffic.

Like the chapel on Wakefield Bridge that on Rotherham Bridge has had a somewhat varied history. It was built in the late fifteenth century and was not endowed; it is possible that the cost of its erection was largely borne by Thomas Rotherham who was Archbishop of York. It was furnished sumptuously, one of its features being an image of Our Lady and the Blessed Babe, 'of gold welwrought'. Gifts from the many travellers who came to pray there as well as bequests maintained the building and paid for the priest who served there.

The chapel survived the dissolution of the monasteries in 1537. After 1547 when the chantries were dissolved the chapel was no longer used for worship but was used again for this purpose during the reign of Mary Tudor, and eventually was converted into an almshouse. By 1681 both the chapel and the bridge, a County bridge, were in a ruinous condition and application was made for repair. There was some demur about whether it was necessary to repair the chapel as well as the bridge but eventually both were agreed to and in all £148, plus £60, plus £20 were granted, separate amounts being estreated.

In 1752 when a survey was made for the *Book of Bridges* the plan and elevation show a bridge of four pointed arches with spans varying between 23 feet and 24 feet and width between parapets of 15 feet. In 1768 the river channel was widened on the western side. The bridge was extended by the addition of a new segmental arch which was 30 feet wide with a width between the parapets of 24 feet 6 inches, so the old bridge was widened to correspond.

At some subsequent date the chapel was in use as a prison but when the new Court House was completed in 1826 this became unnecessary. The bridge, however, became known as 'The Jail Bridge', a name which survived for many years among older residents. The chapel was then let out as a dwelling and, in 1888 became a tobacconist's and newsagent's shop.

By 1901 a thousand inhabitants of Rotherham begged the custodians to restore the chapel but it was not until 1913 that the tobacconist's business was bought out.

The restoration was carried out although not completed until 1924 when, in July, it was reconsecrated for divine worship. By 1921 it was clear that the bridge was becoming increasingly unsafe for the great increase in heavy traffic. A new bridge was built and the old one, now an ancient monument, is a footbridge only.

Ouse Bridge, in York, scene of the miracle in the twelfth century, was, until the building of the bridge at Selby in 1792, the only bridge to cross the River Ouse; there were ferries elsewhere including in the City of York itself, where they remained in use at Lendal and Skeldergate until the bridges were built. There was a bridge in York in Roman times and also in the Middle Ages, a bridge which, by the thirteenth century, was built of stone having houses and shops on it.

In 1564 the bridge collapsed and a temporary ferry was supplied by the Corporation for which the charge was nothing to York citizens, 'Strangers' however were charged a penny per man and horse for both single and return journeys. In less than a year the bridge was rebuilt and in use again. Tolls were collected in order to offset the cost of the bridge from those who passed over it and those who sailed beneath it.

Towards the end of the eighteenth century it was obvious that there was a need for a wider bridge and accordingly an Act of Parliament was sought to give the necessary permission. But there were great delays; differences of opinion about the bridge and financial complications which were not resolved until 1815 when most of the work was made the responsibility of the three Ridings. By 1818 it was possible for pedestrians to cross the bridge but it was not completed until 1820 at a cost of about £80,000. Tolls were collected until 1829. The design was that of Peter Atkinson, the younger.

As York expanded it became increasingly clear that more convenient ways of crossing the river were needed and that the remaining ferries should be replaced by bridges. When York's first railway station was opened the need for a bridge to replace the ferry at Lendal was pressing and in 1838 a company was formed with this in mind. However the idea came to nothing, possibly because of lack of finance. In 1840 the proposal was revived but again nothing definite was achieved. The following year the York and North Midland Railway Company pressed for an improved river crossing at Lendal and although the Corporation gave its collective blessing the scheme was killed by the opposition of shopkeepers in the area of Micklegate and Ouse Bridge. The idea was again resurrected in 1846 this time by George Hudson the Railway King. His suggestion was that a bridge should be jointly financed by York Corporation and the railway company, but again lack of capital killed the idea before it had got off the ground.

In 1859 the scheme was revived yet again and an act was obtained in 1860 giving the necessary permission. Work started almost immediately on a design by the engineer William Dredge but unfortunately the following year when the supports were removed part of the bridge collapsed resulting in the death of five workmen. The sum of £20,745 had already been spent on the bridge. However the Corporation did not want the scheme to drop and asked Thomas Page who was at the time working on the new Westminster Bridge to submit a design. The additional cost was £15,000 and the bridge was opened to traffic in January 1863; tolls were charged until 1894 when the bridge became free of toll.

Lendal Bridge was well used, so well used that a campaign was soon started to replace the ferry at Skeldergate by a bridge. An Act was obtained in 1875 but the work was not started until 1878 and the bridge was opened in 1881. The cost was about £67,000 and tolls were charged until 1914 when the bridge became free.

In the 1770s Selby was becoming increasingly prosperous and there was a need for an improved system of communications. The Leeds-to-Selby Turnpike Act had allowed for the repairing and enlarging of a road between the two towns but the only way of crossing the river was by ferry. It was felt by many local people that there should be a bridge to replace the ferry and by 1788 this had crystallised into definite action. A group of local traders and landowners asked William Jessop to report on the feasibility of this; his report was favourable and so, in 1789, Parliament was approached for the necessary permission.

These local traders and landowners were supported by many of the inhabitants of Selby and also by residents in the surrounding villages all of whom were interested in the possibility of an easier means of access to the town. The Ouse Navigation Trust however thought that a bridge would damage the river trade and also feared that their tolls would diminish; they therefore opposed the idea. Also in opposition were the Earl of Beverley who had interests in three ferries further down the river and a group of landowners who feared that the piers of the bridge would increase danger from flooding.

The two sides agreed to submit the matter to arbitration and to abide by the outcome of the deliberations of the arbitrators, who ultimately reported that they judged a bridge would be of great benefit to the public.

In 1791 the Selby Bridge Act was obtained by which a company was given powers to build and operate the bridge; compensation for the ferry owner was stated and the interests of the Ouse Navigation Trust were safeguarded. Maximum tolls were fixed, 3/-for carts etc. drawn by six horses, 1d for each cow, ½d for each foot passenger. At first the inhabitants of Selby and several nearby villages were allowed to cross free from toll on condition that they made only one trip every twenty-four hours. This became so complicated to administer that eventually all foot passengers crossed free of charge. Measures were also drawn up to protect the interests of shipping.

To make sure that the bridge was properly built the proprietors were obliged to act on the advice of two (or more) engineers selected from a list of distinguished names; these were John Smeaton, William Jessop, Robert Whitworth, John Carr and Thomas Atkinson. The bridge was built fifty yards down the river from where the ferry had crossed for seven hundred years.

It was built almost entirely of timber with large wooden piers; it was a swing bridge and could, from the beginning, be opened in less than a minute. The opening system of the bridge attracted great attention. Rather than open on a drawbridge system which was usual in the eighteenth century, it opened by using a swinging span on a swivel, large ball bearings being used to ensure smooth opening.

The original bridge lasted until 1970 when it was replaced and had it not been for several accidents on the river in the 1960s it may well have lasted longer. The new bridge took about a year to complete at a cost of £125,000. However, 180 years on, the original act shaped the work of the twentieth-century builders. A metal bridge would be more suitable, but, as the act specified a timber bridge, a timber bridge it had to be, although permission was secured to place eight steel girders across the timber deck for extra strength. The timber deck is of Greenheart wood which comes from Ghana and Gambia. According to the terms of the act the company is to support, maintain and keep the bridge and its approaches for ever in good repair.

Another important ferry which crossed the Ouse was that at Cawood. One night the carrier's waggon from York to Cawood was crossing the river by the ferry. It was a windy night and the force of the wind on the cover of the waggon caused the ferry boat to become unmanageable. It was forced downstream where it came into collision with a barge and the waggon, which was full of people, was thrown into the river. Fortunately only one life was lost and that was the carrier, who lost his life because his wife was saved. The two were struggling in the water when a boatman came to their rescue. He grabbed hold of both and pulled but realised that he had only enough strength to save one, not both. He leaned over the side of the boat and said, 'Ah can only save yan, which 'es it to be?' 'Save Bessie', said the carrier.

The iron bridge which was thrown across the Ouse and opened in 1872 has been a great boon to travellers. It was built on the swivel principle with two open spaces of considerable width enabling vessels to pass through it without lowering their sails or casting off their towing ropes. The bridge was built from plans supplied by Mr Robert Hodgson, the engineer to the North West Railway Company.

Local tradition claims a bridge over the Wharfe at Wetherby as early as the Norman era; a bridge which was eleven feet wide. The first mention to be found in contemporary documents is in the visitation of Archbishop Gray where it is stated that on June 18th 1233 the Archbishop granted an indulgence of ten days to last until the next Easter to those who should contribute to the construction of the bridge at Wetherby. This bridge may have been the first one or it may have replaced an earlier one. Pontage was granted for Wetherby Bridge in 1281 and in 1313 Sir William le Vavasour bequeathed twenty shillings for the repair of Wetherby Bridge.

By 1315 the bridge was again in need of repair and the widow of Henry de Perci, Eleanor, who was executrix of the Will of Sir Richard Arundel, petitioned for pontage of Wetherby Bridge which she intended to repair for the soul of Richard Arundel. An inquisition found that in fact nobody was bound to repair the bridge at Wetherby; it is not clear why it was not an obligation on the township. Eleanor was already beginning to repair the bridge and so a grant was made to her of pontage upon all the wares for sale which were carried across the bridge.

In 1378 Richard II granted pontage to 'the good men of Wetherby' for three years. However, other 'good men' coming to or through Wetherby sought to evade the toll due for crossing the bridge by crossing the ford. So, rather more than a year later another grant was made this time including the ford as well as the bridge.

Not far from Wetherby, at Tadcaster, it seems that a bridge had existed 'Time out of memory' as the jurors in 1273 were ignorant as to the origin of the toll which was levied on those who used it. The original bridge was no doubt a narrow structure made of timber. A stone bridge was probably built in the period 1235-45. The cartulary of Healaugh has an entry in which it is recorded that a penalty of two shillings was imposed for the non payment of rent for a tenement in Smaws (near Tadcaster) to be paid to the fabric of the bridge at Tadcaster. Leland spoke of the bridge as containing 'eight fair arches of stone, strengthened by solid rounded buttresses to stay the great pressure of water at flood time.' The bridge was altered to the present width about the middle of the eighteenth century. Leland claimed that the bridge was built from the ruins of Tadcaster Castle.

Two of the most handsome bridges in Yorkshire are those at Castleford and Ferrybridge. In 1485 there was a bequest, in the will of Richard Rawson of Fryston of £20 to be applied in 'amending of Ferybrigge and Catelforth brigge and highweis.' In both cases this would refer to earlier bridges than the present ones, possibly, in the case of Ferrybridge, to that which, in Leland's time, consisted of seven arches. The present bridge is a magnificent structure which was the work of John Carr and

Bernard Hartley of Pontefract. Underneath John Carr's name, which is on one parapet, is the date 1797 and on the other under Bernard Hartley's name is the date 1804.

There are three arches with a small overflow arch at one end and three small overflow arches at the other. There are niches for statues on the bridge and a balustrade on the inside which does not cut right through to the side facing the river. The cutwaters are carried up in one piece right to the parapet. There is a stone at the bottom of the parapet indicating that one half was the responsibility of Brotherton and the other half that of Ferrybridge. I was told by a local man that the foundations of the bridge are placed on bales of wool.

Watling Street crosses the River Aire at Castleford, and, in Roman times there was a ford, possibly paved. Tolls were charged for crossing the ford or ferry and possibly there was no bridge until the fourteenth century. Tradition, however throws a different light on matters, a story recorded by Thomas de Castleford, a Benedictine monk, tells of a miracle whereby the lives of people crossing a wooden bridge at Castleford were saved when the bridge collapsed. Their salvation was brought about by the prayers of a nephew of the wife of King Stephen (1135-54).

It is probable that the cost of building bridges at Castleford and Ferrybridge was borne by the de Laci family who were the Lords of the Honour of Pontefract. The tolls charged for crossing the ford/ferry were probably transferred to the bridge.

This stone bridge was built a little further downstream from the Roman ford and had seven arches. Under the bridges act of 1530 it became an important County bridge. During the latter part of the eighteenth century it became increasingly dilapidated and in 1765 one of the arches was broken. It was partially rebuilt and frequent repairs were necessary to the piers.

Eventually, in 1804 it was demolished and a new bridge built. This new bridge was the work of Bernard Hartley and his son Jesse, it stands still and carries a great deal of traffic; it is an extremely elegant and handsome structure. Bernard Hartley was appointed West Riding Bridge Surveyor, in the late 1790s.

The amazing strength of some of the early bridges, and the quality of the mason work is shown by Catterick Bridge. The River Swale was spanned by a wooden bridge a short distance to the west of the present Catterick Bridge; this was on the Brompton side of Catterick and was the Brompton Brigg which was referred to in early charters.

In 1421 a contract was made between seven local gentry and three masons, Thomas Ampleforthe, John Garrett and Robert Maunsell 'to make a brigg of stane oure ye water of Swalle atte Catrik betwixt ye olde stane brigge and ye Newbrigge of tre (timber) sufficient and workmanly in Masoncraft accordland in substance to Barnacastell brigge.'[10] This bridge was to have two piers and three arches, abutments and parapets and was to be completed in four years for a cost of about £175.

The records of the Quarter Sessions of the North Riding contain grants relating to Catterick Bridge, which amount to more than £1,570 and cover the years 1565-90. In the following century the bridge continued to be a great expense. A 'plaisterer,' John Johnson, undertook repair work and was required to enter into a bond for £260 and to keep the bridge in repair for seven years. Despite this, by 1634 the bridge had cost £588 4 8d, and, by 1674 was in a very ruinous condition.

Since those days a military camp has been established nearby – Catterick Camp. It was not until 1922 that Catterick Steel Girder Railway Bridge was built and until this time the railway track for Catterick Camp ran across the Swale on Catterick Road Bridge. Therefore, a bridge built in the 1420s, having stood nearly five hundred years, carried locomotives of a hundred tons or more.

All bridges are interesting, some for a variety of reasons, are more interesting than others; three which come to mind have a common link in that they seem almost redundant; one in fact so redundant that it has disappeared.

In the centre of Slaithwaite in the Colne Valley is what would be described in a tourist guide as a quaint and attractive bridge. Attractive it certainly is as one catches sight of it when coming down the hill and round the corner from the Manchester road. Standing further back than the river bridge it is quite distinct with its grey stone and hump back: it appears however to be a bridge over nothing. The river, several yards away has a perfectly adequate bridge. From one side this hump back bridge is approached by a road and a packhorse track seems to be the answer. But why doesn't it, or didn't it, cross the river? One walks a little further and the mystery seems solved. This must at one time have been a canal bridge but the canal has been filled in in the town centre, one section ends at this bridge and it is possible to 'pick up' the canal again a couple of minutes walk away.

Not exactly redundant as it carries walkers over a stream they would otherwise have to negotiate as best they may is Thieves Bridge. This looks like a packhorse bridge without its parapet. Located at Standedge just behind the Great Western Hotel it seems to be on a path which goes nowhere and comes from nowhere. In fact the path is one route to and from a section of the Pennine Way. It is not likely to be a pack horse bridge as in all probability it was not built until about 1760. It does not fit in with the line of the old turnpike road being some distance behind it and in any case would have been too narrow for a turnpike bridge. So, although it can be said to have a useful purpose the reason for its existence in the first place is not clear.

Near the site of the bloody and terrible battle of Towton in 1461 is the Cock Beck. At the point where this beck joins the River Wharfe a small bridge was located, Kettleman Bridge. Several writers have spoken of this bridge and its unusual antiquarian interest. Samuel Smiles, quoting another authority seemed to think that the bridge was of Roman origin, a view which has been repeated by Speight, Bogg and Fletcher. It consisted of a single round arch without keystone and was of early construction, the width of the arch being thirteen feet seven inches.

> The stones are squared after the Roman manner and several of them bear old mason marks. The voussoir or wedge shaping of the stones used in the construction of the arch is almost invariably present in Roman bridges as is also the projection of the piers supporting the arch below the springing line.[11]
> Speight

> By some writers the arch of the bridge is supposed to have been Roman work and the name 'Old Street' which passes over it, would almost favour this idea. But the building of the present stone structure cannot be placed earlier than the thirteenth century.[12]
> Bogg

> The arch, springing from square pier walls has no keystone and the blocks of stone of which it is composed resemble, but are larger than, those in the Roman walls at York.[13]
> Fletcher

In 1415 the Dean and Chapter of York granted 3/4 for the construction of a stone staith at Ketilmyrebrygg and in 1432 the sum of 53/4 was disbursed for the carriage of 64 loads of stones from the Minster (at York) Quarries at Huddleston, to

Ketilburnbrig super aquam de Quarf i.e. to Kettleman Bridge on the water of Wharfe. From the bridge the stone was probably taken by water to York.

At the point of confluence of the Cock Beck and the Wharf, the point marked on the map Kettleman Bridge there is a concrete-and-steel structure. Some yards distant there are two low stone walls, apparently quite without purpose.

It seems that these are the parapets of Kettleman Bridge, the bridge itself having been buried during banking work which was carried out about 1970 to control flooding. In the late 1970s further work was done to alter the outflow of the Cock Beck and construct the bridge and sluice gate. This work was the second time the position of the mouth of the Cock Beck has been altered. About 1900 the course of the beck was straightened as there was originally a wide loop in the beck just before it entered the Wharfe. Kettleman Bridge was over one leg of the loop and was certainly visible as late at 1965. At this time it spanned a gully which was dry for much of the time. When the banking work was done about 1970 the gully was filled in, and the bridge buried so that only the parapets remained above ground.

4 Canal Bridges

The turnpike roads and the existing bridges were not adequate to carry the increased amount of traffic made necessary by the economic expansion of the eighteenth century. For centuries rivers had been used for transport, most of the main waterways of England being navigable. Rivers, however, flowed where nature ordained, which was not necessarily where the new industrial areas were developing.

Improvements to river navigation – dredging, deepening, straightening banks, was no new feature of the eighteenth century, nor was the construction of short cuts to join sections of river. But, in England at any rate, the systematic creation of long stretches of water for the purpose of conveying goods, was a new method of transport.

Canal construction brought to prominence certain civil engineers of whom James Brindley, John Smeaton, John Rennie and Thomas Telford are perhaps the best known. The profession of civil engineering was virtually unknown at the time these men were working. But there were millwrights, and it was from this profession – men with an eye for proportion and balance and structure, men who had a natural ability to see how things worked – that the pioneers of canal construction were drawn. Millwrights usually worked with wood but they had opportunities to use other materials, iron for instance, and probably stone, and their varied work gave them the chance to learn, on the job, the strengths and capabilities of the various materials on which they worked.

Smeaton, Brindley and Rennie, all, as children, were absorbed in the use of tools and were never happier than when constructing models of water-wheels, pumps and windmills and harnessing their models to power and seeing them work. The men who rose to eminence as canal engineers and whose names have become familiar to later generations, acted more usually in the capacity of consultants, giving advice, controlling and supervising those who worked under them. In descending order of importance there would be one resident engineer, perhaps more than one, several under engineers, each in charge of a section of the canal, while at the bottom of the pyramid were the masons, carpenters and smiths who built the bridges and locks and the men who dug the earthworks.

Large-scale contracting was practically nonexistent at the time the early canals were built. Work for short sections of a canal would be let to a small firm, agreements being made for labour or materials only, bridges usually being built by those which specialised in masonry. It was unusual to find businesses with sufficient expertise to undertake difficult operations such as laying foundations underwater, but as time went on contracting enterprises grew in size and, with some of the later canal building, it was possible to employ one large firm for all such work. An alternative to employing small contractors was to use direct labour, that is workers employed by the canal company, under the supervision of the engineer.

There were no maps available which in any way approximated to the accuracy of those of the present day Ordnance Survey, although there were some local maps, and so it was a matter of a great deal of legwork on the part of the surveyor to establish the line of a canal. In the early days especially the canals followed long meandering routes in order to avoid the difficulties of making cuttings, embankments and tunnels.

The Pennines presented a major challenge to engineers and two of the three trans-Pennine canals have long tunnels. The Rochdale Canal, however, was built to cross the Pennines without the engineers having to construct one major tunnel. Surveys of the line were made in 1790 and 1791 but the Bill which was presented to Parliament in 1792 as a result of these surveys failed to get sufficient support. The following year a Bill proposing a narrow canal with a 9,000 foot tunnel at the summit, also failed, by only one vote, to gain approval.

The committee called in for consultation the engineer William Jessop who suggested a wide canal in which the summit level should be raised to a greater height by an additional series of seven locks on each side. This new line, which dispensed with the need for a tunnel, was the one which formed the basis for a third

Accommodation bridge described by J. Aiken

Bill in 1794, and which was successful.

Canals, like the railways and motorways which succeeded them, aroused opposition not least from the landowners whose property was affected by their siting. One bone of contention was that a canal sliced through an estate or divided a farm. In many cases this was unavoidable and accommodation bridges were built for the use of local traffic, probably no more than a few horse-drawn carts.

The accommodation bridge in addition to linking two sections of one landholding and enabling traffic to go across the canal, had also to allow fully laden barges to travel freely along it. These bridges were either fixed or movable. Aiken, writing in the early 1790s by which time canals had become quite an accepted feature of British landscape, says, 'Also a canal in its course often divides lands with which some communication is necessary for the purposes of husbandry. The easiest method is shown on Plate IV.'[1] Plate IV in fact shows a canal with a lifting bridge and also, in the near distance, a hump back bridge.

We are told that the lifting bridge hangs by large hooks and eyes – and to women familiar with sewing, and with the old fashioned metal, often black, hooks and eyes on clothing, the vision thus called up is somewhat amusing – and is worked up and down with ease by means of balance poles.

Movable bridges like the 'hook and eye' bridge could be built of wood and may have been easier and cheaper to construct than fixed bridges. Lifting bridges of one type or another were common on the Llangollen canal, there is a good example at Wrenbury; and on the southern part of the Oxford canal.

Swing bridges were also used, these were very common on the Leeds and Liverpool canal, where, in the 1930s they were principally of wood. Many were unlocked, just hooking for security onto an iron bar at the side, and could be swung by anyone, providing free entertainment for children who swung back and forth until ordered off by the lock keeper. These swing bridges linked farmland and also joined two sections of busy main road. Over one such road the local bus company accommodated itself to the needs of the canal and operated a single decker bus rather shorter than the normal size with a long bonnet rather like a pig's snout. It operated between Bingley and Morton and was known locally and affectionately as 'the Morton Pig'.

Many of these swing bridges on the Leeds and Liverpool Canal, and there are a lot, have been reconstructed and the wooden

Canal swing bridge near Clayton-le-Moors

components replaced with metal parapets and metal decks. There is one still near Clayton-le-Moors with a wooden deck. Many are now locked, and cruising parties are provided with a key to enable them to open the bridges.

The Leeds and Liverpool of course is not the only canal with swing bridges, although they are noticeably lacking on the Rochdale. One can still find examples on the Lancaster and on the Huddersfield Narrow where, on the one swing bridge on the Yorkshire side, the wooden deck has two metal strips to reinforce it. The Sheffield and South Yorkshire Canal also has swing bridges.

The fixed hump back bridges so distinctive to canals were originated by Brindley. They are characterised by a wide arch and a slight inward curve from the perpendicular and these two features give an appearance of stability. Distinctive to Brindley's work and that of the engineers who followed his example is the moulded surround of the arch and the keystone. These hump back bridges are architecturally pleasing, and many, especially those in the less urbanised areas are still quite unspoilt and look now much as they must have done when they were first built. The masonry is sound and the workmanship excellent. Unspoilt bridges can be found on all the canals of Yorkshire and Lancashire but are particularly numerous on the Lancaster canal which is in any case the most rural of the canals, and on parts of the Leeds and Liverpool. The needs of expanding urbanisation, especially an increase in the amount and type of traffic using the bridges meant widening and reinforcement. Examples, although these are by no means the only ones, can be seen on the Huddersfield Narrow Canal at Milnsbridge, on bridges in the centre of Brighouse on the Calder and Hebble, and the bridges in Burnley on the Leeds and Liverpool. It is unfortunate that the widening and reinforcement has been carried out in such an ugly way especially as the original bridges, which can be clearly seen under the unsightly cladding, were so graceful. Minor disfiguration has been caused by the siting of a pipe on or near a bridge, the bridge at Swine Lane, near Bingley is an example, also that at the Fisherman Inn in Bingley, while another instance can be seen on a bridge near Garstang.

Construction of the standard canal bridge allowed some flexibility; in many cases the stones forming the arch were left without the addition of a moulded surround and were flush with the main stonework of the arch, as on two of the bridges at Kirkstall on the Leeds and Liverpool Canal, and one at Parson's Walk, Kildwick, also on the Leeds and Liverpool. A present feature of bridges on this canal, whether or not they have this stone moulding is that the arch surround is painted white and the highest point from a navigation point of view, not necessarily the centre point, is marked. On one of the Kirkstall bridges which appears to be of later construction than many of the others, the stone moulding is deeply indented to form a zigzag round the arch.

Many, although not all of the standard bridges have a distinct keystone, and in most cases it is single. That on one of the bridges in the centre of Brighouse is very prominent with the date 1828 carved upon it. The bridges on the Rochdale Canal have a single keystone and those on the Lancaster Canal have a double one. On one of the bridges on the Lancaster Canal the double keystone has been decorated by incised lines forming decreasing oblongs with three parallel lines on the centre part of the keystone and one inner line on the other two parts.

Another feature of the standard canal bridge is a flat-edged parapet and a narrow or rounded buttress at either end with a string course running, usually, right across the top of the arch and from one side of the bridge to the other crossing both buttresses. But there are variations. Two bridges in the middle section of the Lancaster Canal for example are different for several reasons. They are built from a different coloured stone, a stone with a reddish tinge; instead of ashlar they are of rusticated masonry, and they have a single, rather than a double keystone and a rather pointed instead of a flat parapet.

A pointed parapet makes a great difference to the appearance of a bridge giving an altogether more slender and delicate effect. There is a pointed parapet on the bridge at the junction of the Bradford Canal – now defunct – with the Leeds and Liverpool at Shipley, and there is another on the bridge at Parson's Walk, Kildwick. But the most delightful effect of the pointed parapet is to be seen on the lock tail bridges of the Huddersfield Broad Canal, Sir John Ramsden's Canal.

The Deep Cutting bridge on the Lancaster canal retains the shape of the standard canal bridge but has a high arch spring. Near it is the Broken Back bridge. It is obvious why this got its name but not how it came to be broken, and absence of information leaves one free to conjecture. Did eighteenth or early

Deep Cutting bridge

nineteenth century vandals gradually pick away at the masonry until part of the parapet collapsed? Did some unfortunate traveller who had celebrated well but unwisely drive his carriage into the side on his return from his revels? Was some local merchant anxious to see for himself from his vantage point that

Broken Back bridge

his goods were transported punctually and efficiently? Or did,
one wonders naughtily, a Lancastrian equivalent of the

Pickwickian Weller Senior have an accident when, 'as he came down with them woters, his coach *was* upset on that 'ere wery spot, and ev'ry man on 'em was turned into the canal'?[2] Whatever the reason, the repairs, if that is what they are, do not intrude into the landscape. The Lancaster canal also has a bridge with a concave parapet.

Building materials vary from one district to another, the material being determined by what was available in each district or easily imported from an adjacent one. Brick as a building material, even in areas in which its use is common, can be harsh and glaring. But many of the brick canal bridges have mellowed with age and melt into their background, for example that at Somerton on the Oxford canal and Winson Green on the B.C.N. Most of the standard bridges on the Yorkshire and Lancashire canals are of stone, although bricks have been used and they are not, as one might expect, intrusive. On the Huddersfield Narrow canal there is a bridge which is built entirely of blue brick while near Elland on the Calder and Hebble there is a stone bridge which has a red brick parapet. Described thus briefly it sounds very unattractive but in fact this bridge, particularly with the sun shining on it seems warm and mellow and blends well into the landscape.

The rise to prominence of canals as a means of transport roughly coincided with an expansion of the iron industry and the iron foundries supplied cast iron bridges to the canal companies. Many are extremely attractive, for example that over the Newport Pagnall branch of the Grand Junction Canal; the bridge which once carried the Neath Abernant Tramroad across the River Cynon at Robertstown, Aberdare; and the roving bridge at the junction with Lord Hay's branch canal on the Wyrley and Essington Canal.

The Yorkshire and Lancashire canals are not noted for their graceful iron, or perhaps eventually steel, bridges, iron being apparently used to reinforce the brick and stonework as decay and dilapidation have taken place; two examples of this being the Huddersfield Narrow canal where the metal parapets are smartly painted and bear the dates 1861 in one case and 1884 in the other. There is a similar reinforcement on a bridge on the Lancaster canal not far from the town centre which bears the name of the ironfounder. The metal arch parapet on one of the bridges near Brighouse on the Calder and Hebble canal is especially lacking in

Canal turnover bridge

grace, although in the centre of the town itself the bridge with its lattice work parapet is quite attractive. There is on the Huddersfield Broad canal an iron bridge which is quite unique on the British canal system. This is the iron locobridge, a lifting bridge on which the whole platform of the bridge is raised upwards. It was built in the early 1860s and bears the date 1865.

Roving, crossover, turnover, snake or changeling, are words apparently interchangeable which describe a bridge which was built at a point where it was necessary to change the towpath from one side of the canal to the other. Such a bridge enabled the horse and towrope to move from one section of towpath to another without the necessity of unhitching the towrope. This situation also occurred at the junction of two canals and correctly speaking the term roving bridge should only be applied to a bridge which was built at such a junction. A particularly good example of a roving bridge is in Shipley where the now defunct and filled in Bradford canal joins the Leeds and Liverpool. A very small portion of the Bradford canal, beloved by fishermen, remains at this point. Examples of a turnover bridge are on the Lancaster canal near the boat moorings in the town centre, on the Leeds and Liverpool canal near the aqueduct at Dowley Gap, and

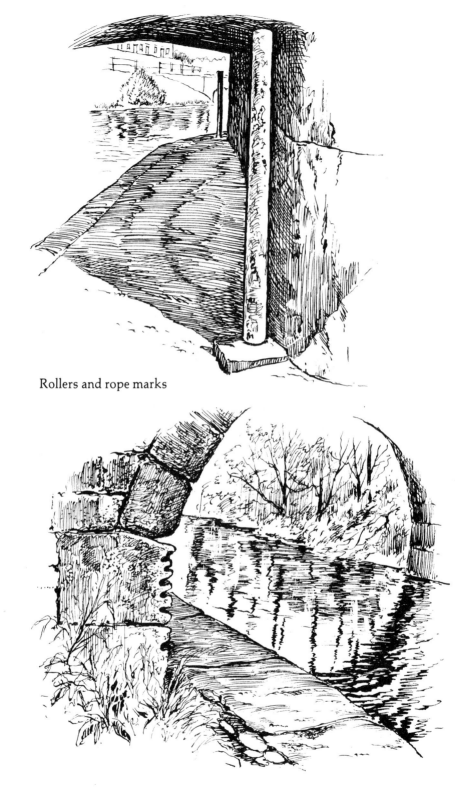

Rollers and rope marks

near Nelson, just below Barrowford locks.

The split bridge was another way which was devised to dispense with the need to unhitch the rope when the bridge was without a towpath. The two arms of the bridge were moved apart allowing the rope to be passed through the gap in the middle. There is an example of a split bridge at Yarningdale on the Stratford canal.

The presence of locks made it necessary to provide bridges for the boatmen to go from one side of the canal to the other to operate them. Those on the Rochdale canal are superb, with a buttress at one end and at the other the parapet sloping down and round so there was no projection to catch the towing lines. In recent reconstruction work, wooden footbridges are being built similar to those in use on the Leeds and Liverpool. On the Calder and Hebble and the Huddersfield Broad canals there are wooden platforms at the back of the lock gates. By far the ugliest and crudest lock tail bridge is that at the junction of the Huddersfield Broad canal with the Calder and Hebble at Cooper bridge. It is modern, and perhaps expedience and economy have, in its construction, been more important than artistry, which is a great pity as it devalues the other splendid and graceful bridges on the canal.

There are reminders too on our canals that in the heyday of canal commercial usage boats were powered by horses; grooves which have been worn at the edge of the bridges can be seen in several places and are due to the constant rubbing by the towrope. In order to reduce or stop this, rollers were placed at the edge of the arch to take the strain of the rope, and these can still be seen on some bridges, at Burnley where both are in place, at the Fisherman Inn bridge, Bingley, at Hebden Bridge and on the Calder and Hebble canal near Elland.

One of the most interesting bridges is that at Marton on the Leeds and Liverpool canal. This is, in fact, the standard canal bridge doubled, with one bridge on top of another. It was built thus simply because the contractor wanted to make quite sure that his bridge was of sufficient strength to take the weight of traffic.

Bridge building, although it called for some skill and ingenuity on the part of canal engineers did not present much of a challenge. On all canals it was inevitable that somewhere along the line it would cross a wide valley, a stream or a river, and bridging such gaps called for engineering expertise. Aqueducts

Marton Bridge

were not new, the Romans had used them, but they were new in Britain.

It was James Brindley who was approached by John Gilbert, the Duke of Bridgewater's agent, and asked to cut a canal to carry coal from the Duke's coal mines at Worsley, to Manchester. Brindley surveyed a route and in 1760 the necessary Act was passed to enable the Duke to carry his proposed canal over the River Irwell near Barton Bridge. Crossing the Irwell was an extremely ambitious scheme and was, in some quarters, considered wild and impossible. To build a channel of water high in the air and sail ships along it above other ships which were sailing on the river below was thought to be the scheme of a madman. The Duke was advised that to proceed with such a scheme would merely be a waste of money and Brindley was urged to think again about the advisability of his plan. So insistent were the critics that the Duke called in a second engineer, probably, although not certainly, John Smeaton. While Brindley refused to compromise, his idea was dismissed by Smeaton (if indeed it was he) as unworkable and unsound. The Duke however was loyal to his engineer, backed his hunch and allowed Brindley to continue.

The Barton aqueduct, built by Brindley, entirely of stone blocks, was about 600 feet in length and 36 feet wide. The centre part was sustained by a bridge of three semicircular arches, the middle arch having a 63 foot span. Carrying the canal across the River Irwell at a height of 39 feet above the river it did indeed appear to be, as Brindley's critics had derisively described it, a 'Castle in the air'. It was a bold and worthy enterprise and pointed the way for later magnificent canal aqueducts and railway viaducts. At the time of its construction it was unique in England and attracted a great deal of attention.

The ingenious Brindley faced a twofold problem. Not only had his aqueduct to be structurally sound enough to bear the weight of water but it also needed to be watertight.

In order to ensure complete retention of water Brindley used puddle. Puddle is formed from a mixture of sand and clay which is reduced to a semi fluid state by being chopped about with spades. The thick syrupy liquid was then plastered in at least three layers to a thickness of about three feet, care being taken that each layer should blend with its predecessor so that there were no nicks or crevices through which water could seep. A layer of soil was usually laid over the last course.

There are some fine aqueducts large and small such as Brynich on the Brecon and Abergavenny canal; Dundas on the Kennet and Avon canal; Marple on the Peak Forest canal; Pont Cysyllte on the Llangollen canal; Another fine aqueduct not dissimilar from that at Barton was the Barnsley aqueduct over the River Dearne. It was a five-arched masonry structure upon which Jessop decided in June 1794 instead of an embankment and culvert. A drawing of it shows its substantial piers and cutwaters and its five segmental arches with strip buttresses and two string courses. The aqueduct has now been demolished but the remnants of the piers have been used to support a footbridge in the new Dearne Park which has fairly recently been opened.

One of Brindley's plain, solid, uncompromising, but not unpleasing aqueducts carries the Leeds and Liverpool canal over the River Aire at Dowley Gap. This consists of seven segmental arches each having its stones flush with the masonry of the main wall and no moulded surround. The aqueduct is very like that over the River Sow on the Staffordshire and Worcester canal. The plans for the Dowley Gap aqueduct were prepared by Brindley and the contracting work was let to Jonathan Sykes of Oulton and Joseph Smith of Woodlesford who were masons.

The aqueducts on the Leeds and Liverpool canal are very similar to one another. That over the Eshton Beck at Gargrave is like that at Dowley Gap but smaller, having only five arches, the arch stones having reticulated masonry which gives a dimpled effect. There are two string courses, one just above the arches but not touching them, and another just below the parapet, and they too have this dimpled effect. There are no cutwaters.

At either end of the aqueduct there is a buttress which comes only to the top of the upper string course. Smaller but again very similar are the three arched aqueduct at Priestholme at the other side of Gargrave and the two arched aqueduct near Barrowford locks. This has rounded cutwaters and the masonry is punched giving this very pleasing dimpled effect.

There is another two-arched aqueduct in Thompson Park in Burnley carrying the canal over the River Brun. Under one of its arches is a paved path which is a busy pedestrian thoroughfare to and from the town centre, and many of those who use it must be unaware that they are walking under a piece of history. The two arches do not appear to be identical in size, the eastern one seems slightly wider than that at the west and also less steep. The stone moulding round the arches and the spandrel walls are rusticated and punched giving a dimpled effect. There is a broad string course across the aqueduct above the arches in hammer-dressed masonry, not rusticated, and higher still a narrower string course. There is a projecting edge above the centre of the two arches carrying the string course outwards, and the effect of this, along with the rustication, is to give an impression of solidarity.

Culverts are rather different from aqueducts although they serve the same purpose. At Kildwick the Leeds and Liverpool canal is carried across the road by a culvert. Walking underneath it is dank and unpleasant with a chilly gloomy atmosphere, the walls are damp and while there is no fear of the water rushing through, one always feels pleased to be out of it and safely at the other side.

There was another culvert built in 1796 which carried the same canal across one of the main roads in Burnley; this was rather like a standard canal bridge with a higher parapet. As time went on and traffic into and out of Burnley increased this was too narrow and various schemes were suggested to widen it. This was not done but two smaller arches, one at either side and intended for pedestrians, were added in 1896 and 1897. In 1926 the culvert was replaced by the present aqueduct, in many ways the most impressive along the line of the canal. It is built in stone with a metal trough. There is a parapet of lattice stonework with deep sides, the decorations being in pseudo-triumphal Roman style. The main motifs are a lion's head with a wreath in its mouth and a wreath of laurel supported on a Doric column with crossed ribbons.

The Leeds and Liverpool aqueducts, apart from that over Yorkshire Street in the centre of Burnley, have a family resemblance. Others, resembling quite a different family are those on the Lancaster canal. Originally there were twenty-two of them and, although a definite link is apparent in many of them, they do differ in detail. Characteristic is a concave arc with wide wing walls to take the pressure from the embankment, and a segmental arch, while on some, V-jointed masonry enhances their substantial appearance.

On the aqueduct in Haslam Park in Preston the base of the segmental arch turns inwards rather in the manner of a horse shoe arch, unlike that at Woodplumpton, although both have the common characteristic of V-jointed masonry.

There is no apparent arch on the aqueduct over the River Calder, although there is a string course at the bottom of the main retaining wall. One of the wing walls juts out slightly from the central wall and the parapet is formed by two courses of stone; the whole has regular jointing.

The River Conder aqueduct is different from the other three although it is recognisable as belonging to the same family. Like the others it has the concave arc with the central retaining wall and the substantial wing walls, but it is altogether more square and substantial. At either end of the wing walls there is a buttress

Brock aqueduct

which has been squared off at the top. Across the apex of the arch
is a string course with another at the top of the wall. The parapet
curves round slightly so that the square buttress tops come below
it; there is regular rather than V-jointed masonry.

Three of the most striking aqueducts on the canal, apart from
that over the River Lune, are those at Brock, Hollowforth and that
over the Wyre at Garstang. The river, at the site of the Brock
aqueduct is almost at the same level as the canal so the crossing
was made by building a deep weir over which the river fell into a
channel which had been made by deepening the river bed. There
is a concave arc of masonry with an elliptical course of stone and
two elliptical parallel walls.

The Hollowforth aqueduct is one which bears no family
resemblance to the rest of the aqueducts. There are three
barrel-shaped arches each of which is at the end of a
barrel-shaped tunnel, which runs right underneath the canal.
There are no cutwaters, the masonry is V-jointed and the entire
structure looks solid, substantial and very pleasing. Underneath
one of the arches is a plank to enable the curious to walk under
the aqueduct from one side of the canal to the other.

The Wyre aqueduct at Garstang is, like many of the others
concave but it is much bigger and the concave structure is broken

Hollowforth aqueduct

Wyre aqueduct

by a section of vertical wall above the arch which emphasises the impression of weight and solidity. Architecturally it is superb; there is an entablature of architrave, frieze, cornice and parapet and the courses of stone are alternated between rusticated masonry and hammer-dressed stone. The arch is segmental with a string course round it. Stone as a medium for building is shown at its best here with the alternating courses of differently dressed stone which varies in colour from a sandy shade, through a creamy golden to a delicate grey.

The greatest aqueduct on the Lancaster canal is that over the River Lune at Lancaster. When Rennie prepared his plans for this he seems to have favoured a brick construction but he was overruled by the committee who preferred a stone one. Alexander Stevens and Son of Edinburgh were appointed contractors for it and on 26 July 1793 the specification for the aqueduct was signed by John Rennie and Alexander Stevens. In January 1794, William Cartwright was appointed assistant resident engineer with special responsibility for the foundations. By July that year, 150 men were at work day and night on the undertaking. In August 1795 the company reported that work on the aqueduct was up to the spring of the arches and claimed it was 'the greatest piece of work of its kind in the kingdom'. Alexander Stevens died in January 1796, a loss felt personally by Rennie himself who wrote,

Lune aqueduct

I most sincerely lament the death of poor Stevens. His loss will be felt by us all. In him the company have lost the best of Contractors and I a friend on whose advice I could always rely. I therefore with you most sincerely drop a tear to his memory and had my engagements been fewer than they are I should have come to Lancaster to assist in performing the last office his friends can do. I hope his son will soon arrive and that he will endeavour to follow the footsteps of a Father who has gone through life with so much credit to himself.[3]

Work on the aqueduct was continued by his son and it was opened in November 1797. It was not long before disaster struck, for in September 1798 Cartwright reported to the canal committee that there was 'serious failure at the Lune Embankment on Sunday morning ... it appears that the puddle first gave way in the bottom'. Apparently 216,000 cubic feet of earth were washed away and Cartwright thought it would take six-and-a-half weeks to repair. Five days later he reported that there were fifty-five men and fourteen horses at work in repairs to the embankment.

Disaster of another kind came many years after Cartwright's death which occurred in 1804. In 1820 an advertisement appeared offering a reward of 20 guineas for the discovery of some persons who had wantonly and maliciously broken the balusters of the canal embankment.

All in all the aqueduct was an expensive piece of engineering. It took five years to build, Rennie's original estimate was £18,618 18s 0d which was later amended to £27,500 0s 0d, while the final work was in excess of £48,000. The labourers were paid 2/- per day, the gangers 2/6 and 2/2 and the carpenters 2/6.

There remained the problem of crossing the River Ribble and it was intended that this too should be crossed by a stone aqueduct. When however the northern section from Tewitfield to Preston had been completed and also the southern section from Wigan, the company found that most of its money had been spent. Goods were taken by road across the intermediate area between both ends of the two sections of canal. In July 1799 Cartwright gave his estimate for building locks, an embankment and an aqueduct. This was for £172,945, and, as an intermediate measure he suggested that a tramroad, costing £60,000 should be built to connect the two sections of the canal. Although an Act of Parliament was obtained to allow the company to do this opinions were divided. The original promoters, who were mainly Lancaster merchants interested in increasing the town's trade, had got what they wanted, a canal to Lancaster. The idea of a tramroad had no particular appeal to them, nor to a second group, the Westmorland group who wanted cheap coal in Kendal. Nor did the tramroad appeal to a third group who pointed out that the aqueduct over the Lune was comparatively little used, the major part of the traffic going to Lancaster town. They wanted a through canal with an aqueduct across the Ribble and thought that the building of a tramroad would delay this.

Cartwright had not suggested that the tramroad should be permanent and John Rennie wrote to the Clerk of the Company, Samuel Gregson, pointing out that it was only a temporary expedient. By March 1801 the company was still undecided and Rennie and William Jessop were asked to submit a report on the matter. They reported that a stone aqueduct was the only permanent solution to crossing the Ribble but that, as an interim measure, they recommended the tramroad.

The company bought land and, in order to understand more fully the working of a tramroad Cartwright visited Derbyshire to study that in the Peak Forest. In the construction of the Lancaster canal tramroad large quantities of iron were used, each tramplate had to be cast in the best quality pig iron, had not to exceed the weight of 40 pounds per yard and had to comply with specific measurements and in addition nails or spikes were used to fasten the plates to the sleepers. Stone was also required in large quantities and was supplied from a quarry near Lancaster.

By May 1803 10,500 blocks had been prepared at 5d each. Delays were caused by the unsatisfactory quality of some of the iron plates and by the late delivery of others, but in June 1803 the *Blackburn Mail* reported,

On the first instant, a Boat laden with coal was navigated on the Lancaster Canal thro' the Tunnel at Whittle Hills, and her cargo was discharged into waggons at the termination of the canal at Walton. Twenty-seven waggons were laden, each containing about one ton, and were drawn by one horse, a mile and a half, along the rail road, to the works of Messrs Claytons at Bamber Bridge. The waggons extended one hundred yards in length along the rail road. Geo. Clayton of Lostock Hall Esq., rode upon the first waggon and the tops of the others were fully occupied. The intention of navigating a boat through the Tunnel, upon this day, was not generally known; it was quickly circulated; old and young left their habitations and employments to witness a sight so novel, and before the boat reached her discharging place, she was completely crowded with passengers, who anxiously rushed into her at every bridge. The workmen were regaled with ale at Bamber Bridge; and among the toasts of the party were given, 'The glorious First of June', 'The Memory of Lord Howe', and 'The healths of the surviving heroes of that memorable day.[4]

The incline was worked on an endless chain and as chains frequently broke it was a costly and time consuming matter to repair or replace them. Also costly was the maintenance of the permanent way and so the tramroad proved to be an expensive item. In 1805 the matter of an aqueduct was revived and again opinions differed. Lancaster and Westmorland merchants were in favour of the canal being extended to Kendal, arguing that the tramroad could 'carry on' a little longer. In 1817 the supporters of a Ribble aqueduct tried again but this time the Lancaster and Westmorland group had their sights set on extending the canal to Glasson Dock as soon as the Kendal Canal was finished (it was completed in 1819). A final attempt was made by the supporters to secure a Ribble aqueduct but this was defeated and the matter was finally dropped.

Another of Rennie's aqueducts is that over the Rochdale Canal at Hebden Bridge. It is similar in some respects to that of the Leeds and Liverpool canal at Dowley Gap. There are four segmental arches and the design is low rather than lofty, but here the similarity ends. The arches which have prominent keystones spring from cutwaters above which are plain rectangular buttresses. At present the whole is a uniform dark colour but originally it was a splendid affair due to the use of different stone. Some nut brown stone was used; while the string courses and keystones of the arches were of a pale primrose material and much of the rest in a dark olive green stone.

There is a fine aqueduct on the Huddersfield Narrow Canal. It has a wide concave masonry wall, a segmental arch which is quite unadorned, there are buttresses and a horizontal string course across the top of the arch and another at the top of the aqueduct.

Quite a different aqueduct from any of the others is that which crosses the Aire and Calder canal at Stanley Ferry near Wakefield. This appears to have been designed by George Leather as a plan of his in 1827 seems to suggest that the aqueduct should have a structure of lattice work and an iron trough and six piers. In 1828 Telford stated that at first he had approved of Leather's design

Stanley Ferry aqueduct

but later he and Leather had rejected it favouring a design with a single arch. In April 1834, Leather was told to prepare plans for it and in November the contract was let – for a cast-iron structure – and the foundation stone was laid on 12 May 1837.

The cost was between £40,000 and £50,000. The aqueduct has two bow string girders which support the waterway by means of suspension rods. The tank measures 180 feet by 24 feet by 9 feet and with the water at a depth of 8 feet 6 inches holds 940 tons. The opening of the aqueduct on 15 August 1839 was an occasion for great rejoicing. The *Wakefield Journal* for 16 August had a full report:

Yesterday there was a gay and animated scene at Stanley on the occasion of the opening of the remainder of the new canal from Broadreach, below the Lodge Farm, to Fairies Hill. The water was turned on at Broadreach Lock at three o'clock on Wednesday afternoon and it was an interesting sight to witness the process of filling, which occupied from three to four hours, during which time, as a matter of course, the water in the river below the lock fell several inches, exhibiting here and there a variety of shoals. The canal, when full, altered much the appearance of the scene, affording as it does an attractive sight in the chasm in which it flows. Taking it altogether there is not perhaps, a finer canal in the kingdom.

The first vessel into the cut was the James, she was crowded with persons of various classes who were anxious to have the opportunity of saying that they were in the first vessel in the cut. She was drawn by three grey horses, with outriders, bedecked in blue and other gay colours ... the aqueduct was entered about three o'clock amid tremendous cheering.[5]

The aqueduct formed part of the longer section of the canal to which the passage alludes. It was built by Messrs Graham Milton Ironworks at Elsecar. It is a gracious and unusual aqueduct and has itself now become redundant.

Unique for its ugliness is that which carries the Calder and Hebble canal over a stream at Salterhebble. Its parapets are metal rails which are painted white and they are the only attractive feature of the whole aqueduct. At first sight it seems decrepit and makeshift although closer examination reveals it as apparently sound. There are stone wing walls at either side of the frontal retaining structure, at the top of which, supporting the parapet rails are horizontal wooden planks. Below these can be seen the seven ends of the beams which are laid at right angles to the top planks. Another layer of wood separates these from nine upright wooden beams which rest on an iron girder at the bottom. Two iron girders acting as struts support the structure against the wing walls.

Less spectacular than aqueducts but probably even more taxing on the ingenuity, and certainly more dangerous to construct, were tunnels. As in other matters of canal engineering Brindley was the pioneer. It was, of all things, at a wedding breakfast that Brindley's engineering acumen was discussed. John Heathcote, the owner of the Clifton estate between Manchester and Bolton was married to a daughter of Sir Nigel Gresley of Knypersley near Burslem. He was anxious to find someway of draining water from

Foulridge tunnel

the coal mines on his estate. Brindley was sent for and, on hearing
the problem considered it in silence for some time. His solution
was simple and ingenious but previously untried. It was to use the
fall of water in the River Irwell on the boundary of the estate to
pump water from the pits – an exercise made possible because of
the greater power of the water in the river.

This scheme needed a tunnel which was the first Brindley had built and which he drove through solid rock for 1,800 feet. Into the tunnel the water from the river was channelled onto the breast of a water wheel which was fixed some 30 feet below the surface of the ground. From the lower end of the wheel the water flowed into the lower level of the Irwell.

Tunnels as such, were not new as they had been used in connection with the mining industry for some time, but in these there was rarely any relationship with the surface and the majority were not destined to go in any fixed direction. Brindley's techniques pioneered in that his tunnels had to proceed in a straight line in a fixed direction and at a certain level. In addition to excavating from each end, vertical shafts were also sunk and pumps were erected over each shaft to keep the water clear of the tunnelling.

There are three major tunnels on the Yorkshire and Lancashire canals, the Foulridge and Gannow on the Leeds and Liverpool, and Standedge on the Huddersfield Narrow. The Foulridge tunnel is 4,920 feet long. In 1789 Robert Whitworth estimated that £169,818 was needed to complete the canal. This money included the summit tunnel at Foulridge which he said, compared with what had been done in other canals, 'will be a small affair'. His calculations from his surveys of the ground led him to believe that, 'it will be easier to make than most that have been executed'.

Subsequent events are depressingly familiar and serve to remind us that there is nothing new – public works always seem to cost more than the original estimates. Costs invariably rise, never fall. By 1791 work on the tunnel was behind schedule and doubts began to arise about the wisdom of having a tunnel at all. A second opinion was therefore sought from Josiah Clowes who had been resident engineer in charge of building Sappington tunnel on the Thames and Severn Canal and had also superintended the construction of the Dudley tunnel. In his opinion a tunnel of 900-1,200 feet would have been sufficient but as 2,400 feet of the proposed Foulridge tunnel had already been dug it would be sensible to continue with it.

The tunnel was opened in May 1796 having taken five years to complete and at great expense, parts having cost as much as £8 per foot. There was no towpath in the tunnel and boats were legged through; by the late 1870s as many as ninety each week and in 1880 a tug was ordered for Foulridge tunnel. Legging still continued and in 1882 a legger was killed through suffocation

Gannow tunnel and mason marks

after which legging was prohibited.

As with Foulridge tunnel so with Standedge; matters which appeared simple at the outset took longer to deal with and turned out more and more expensive than had been bargained for.

Standedge canal tunnel

Tunnelling took place from both ends and also from vertical shafts which were sunk from the top of the hill. By 1796 4,455 feet of small subsidiary tunnel had been dug, fourteen pits had either already been dug or were in the process of being dug and one large and three small steam engines had been installed. But only 2,385 feet of the main tunnel had been cut. It was not until 1809 that the two ends of the tunnel were joined and not until March 1811 that it was finished and navigable. The following week there was a ceremonial opening during which a party of about five hundred entered the tunnel to the strains of 'Rule Britannia'. There was a crowd of ten thousand to see the opening ceremony.

The canal had cost just over £400,000 of which the tunnel cost about £160,000 by far the costliest canal tunnel in Britain. Originally it was 16,368 feet long and is now 17,094 feet, nine feet high and nine feet wide. It has been described as a rat hole at the Yorkshire side, and certainly it looks like it, it is difficult to imagine anything less inviting.

The tunnel had no towpath and so boats had to be legged through, an operation for which labourers were hired specially. There seemed to be no lack of men willing to do this which was an unpleasant and dangerous job being performed in total darkness, but they appear to have stayed for only a few days after which they were paid off and went elsewhere to seek casual work. These men were called leggers as they literally worked the boat with their legs kicking it from one end of the tunnel to the other, two leggers in each boat lying on their sides back-to-back using their feet against the opposite walls. Legging was not unique to Standedge being used also at Foulridge and Gannow. The horses were taken over the top. At Gannow there is a path called Boat Horse Lane which was the route over which the horses were taken.

5   Railway Bridges

And so we come to the last wave of bridge building before the motorway age of the later twentieth century – railway bridges. It has been said that the history of bridge building reflects the development of civilization and there seems to be some truth in this: the progress from simple beam bridge to longer clapper bridge to single-arch bridge and ultimately to bridges of several piers with cutwaters shows the development of man's skill in engineering.

As time went on there was a greater variety of materials available for bridge construction. The development by Henry Cort, in 1783 and 1784 of the puddling and rolling processes and the reverberatory furnace enabled wrought iron to be more easily and cheaply produced, which led to its increased use in bridge building. Henry Bessemer's converter (1856) and the open hearth system of Sir William Siemens (1866) were methods of producing steel in quantity and cheaply and this too could be used in bridge building. But a bridge, like any other building, must be efficient, practical and at the same time graceful and well proportioned: many bridges are. Those bridge builders who heeded, albeit unconsciously, Ruskin, who said, 'When we build, let us think that we build for ever',[1] have bequeathed a heritage of grace and beauty; in other cases, some of the iron girder bridges for instance, they have at best created works of tolerable mediocrity and at worst downright ugliness.

That bridge building reflects the development of civilisation is possibly true; that different types of bridges co-exist in a particular place is often a response to the peculiarities of topography rather than an indication of progress. In Wycoller, (the district is known as the valley of the seven bridges), in the vicinity of the hamlet itself, there are the Clam bridge, the clapper bridge and the packhorse bridge. The Clam bridge, a single slab

spanning a narrow stream, is eminently suitable for that particular location. However skilful man had been at the time of its construction there would have been no purpose in making a more elaborate structure.

Nevertheless it is interesting to consider the different bridges which co-exist in a place and see the stages in economic development which they reflect. Linton-in-Craven has a clapper bridge, a packhorse bridge and also a late-nineteenth-century bridge which carries motor vehicles. In Hebden Bridge there is the sixteenth-century packhorse bridge, flanked, downstream and upstream by nineteenth-century road bridges. Marsden, at the head of the Colne Valley is perhaps a more interesting example; still referred to as a village it has no less than twelve bridges. Among these there is the packhorse type bridge which spans the infant river in the centre of the village near the church, and across which in times past hill farmers came to attend church and to bring their grain to be ground at the manorial corn mill. Hoisted across their shoulders or on the back of a packhorse they carried their pieces of cloth to be fulled or taken to market. Beyond this there is Close Gate Bridge taking the packhorse track across the

Carlisle railway bridge at Lancaster, c. 1846

hills into Lancashire. The Colne Valley has, from very early times, and through succeeding centuries, been an important communication link between Yorkshire and Lancashire. The roads crossed the Pennines but when, in later years, the canals and railways came, ways had to be found of cutting through the hills; first a canal tunnel, afterwards a single-bore railway tunnel and, later still when this was found not to be adequate, another bore to enable double track operation. There is also in the village an iron foot-bridge and Ottiwell's Bridge, a stone bridge which was built by John Metcalf in 1780 or 1781.

Economic growth can be traced in Lancaster and Preston from the sequence of bridge building. There was a wooden bridge which crossed the Lune at Lancaster at some time earlier than the thirteenth century, and for several centuries wood was the principal building material. Eventually the bridge was built from stone but increasing traffic in the eighteenth century caused its decay to such an extent that it was considered more expedient to replace it with a new one. The magnificent Skerton Bridge was completed in 1787 almost ten years before the aqueduct on the canal was opened. The tradition of fine building was maintained when, later, the railway was taken across the river. There were two fine viaducts built by the Lancaster and Carlisle Railway Company and the Little North Western Railway Company.

Lune aqueduct

The Act sanctioning the railway from Lancaster to Carlisle was passed in April 1844. Difficulties other than those of engineering beset the engineers who needed to cross the River Lune near Lancaster. Their undertakings were further downstream than the aqueduct and any scheme to build a railway bridge was likely to come into conflict with the interests of the Port Commissioners who would brook no interference from rivals. They were very anxious that their work would not be impeded by the railway company and any bridge which was built. In July 1844 a committee of the Lancaster Port Commissioners was formed to decide how far they could give their assent or dissent to the railway crossing the river and also to ascertain the amount of compensation to be asked, if any. This committee estimated the compensation at £20,000 and stated that the arch of the viaduct was not to be less than thirty-three feet above the level of the quay. A deputation of quay commissioners met some of the directors of the railway company in August when a cat and mouse act was played out. The company offered £12,500 as compensation for crossing the Lune. The commissioners offered to modify their terms to £18,000. However Mr Swift, the solicitor of the railway company, then wrote to say that the directors declined to pay £18,000. Eventually a sum of £16,500 was agreed on. It was on 21 September 1846 that the bridge was opened. It was a stone, timber and trestle structure comprising three laminated arches of 120-foot span each built of timber, and six more, smaller, arches built of stone. It was an impressive engineering feature and the engineers were Messrs Locke and Errington and the contractors Messrs Stephenson, Mackenzie and Brassey. It was later replaced by an iron bridge.

One of the most interesting viaducts on any of the railways built in Britain was that of the 'Little North Western Railway' which carried the line over the River Lune. The portion of this line from Wennington to Lancaster including the viaduct, was opened in 1849 and the *Illustrated London News* carried an interesting description of it – enthusiastic crowds waved banners from every corner of vantage. The viaduct is described as a 'singular structure'.

At the Lancaster end of the portion just opened, and carrying a continuation of the line to Poulton across the River Lune is a timber viaduct. Spanning the river diagonally, and (to suit the exigences of the line of which it forms a part) in the form of a segment, it is of a length much greater than the width of the river being 620 feet over all and thus combines in itself two features of bridge architecture, which, before the commencement of railway works were rarely met with, the curve and the skew – the former being in this case one of 590 feet radius and the latter at an angle of 40 degrees. We believe no other structure has these two features in combination so markedly developed. It has ten openings of sixty feet each over which the road is partly upheld by pile piers and partly suspended from lancinated arches.

The piers consist of clustered piles, presenting the least possible obstruction to the flow of the water, and having an appearance so light in proportion to the mass they have to support that persons unable to appreciate the strength of a structure acquired by skilful combination and disposition of its •parts are apt to arrive at conclusions as to its stability the reverse of true. This was fully exemplified immediately after the bridge was completed. In consequence of the simultaneous occurrence of a strong, fresh and high tide, the water in the river attained a height unexampled for many previous years. A great number of people, spite of the rain collected on the banks, expecting to see the light looking supports of the bridge borne down and the whole fabric carried away by the force of the river current and the receding tide. It is needless to add their expectations were not realised.

From the tops of the piles – their ends resting on cast iron shoes – spring arches formed of three inch planks in layers bent to the required form over temporary centres. There are three of these arches or ribs in the width of the bridge, one on each side and one in the centre.

The roadway is a little above the spring of the arches, and, consequently does not rest upon, but is suspended from, them. Strong iron bolts, or suspension rods (each equal to a strain of twenty tons) are the efficient though, as they pass through upright timbers – invisible instruments used to sustain in suspension over the river the iron road and ponderous trains.

The peculiarities we have described were the result of necessity, not choice, and we think no plan can be devised on which to build a bridge that would be more perfect in its adaptation than the present structure. As a proof of its great strength and promise of stability we may mention that under pressure of 98 tons concentrated upon one arch, when tested under the inspection of Captain Wynne, Government inspector, and J. Watson Esq. C.E. the deflection was only five eighths of an inch.[2]

The slimline and very elegant structure was known locally as the Greyhound Bridge although nobody seems to know why. A logical and suitable explanation seems to be that its lean and elongated appearance is suggestive of the physique of a greyhound – but this is purely conjecture.

This timber viaduct was subsequently replaced. On Saturday, 14 May 1864, the *Lancaster Gazette* reported the opening of the new Greyhound Bridge, 'we are glad to have to announce that the new iron bridge over the Lune on the Morecambe Line is now so far completed that trains run regularly over it. The first train passed over on Wednesday and the traffic over the old wooden bridge is now nearly discontinued.'

The Greyhound Bridge, *c.* 1840

Less than two months later there was another report on this bridge, of which the citizens of Lancaster were very proud –

> We are glad to learn that the authorities are not willing to allow our beautiful new bridge to be any further disfigured by the erection of the prison like wall which has been commenced by the Midland Railway Company and intended by them as a screen to obviate the dangerous nuisance so long complained of. The work on this unsightly wall has been stopped and we understand that a meeting of the parties concerned is to take place on Tuesday next with a view to the adoption of some plan for removing the nuisance without disfiguring the bridge.[3]

The name, although not the bridge has been retained. The 1864 bridge has been removed and in place of it there is a modern road bridge which is still called the Greyhound Bridge.

In the vicinity of Preston there were, in the early centuries ferries and fords, and then, for many years, a wooden, later a stone bridge at Walton, a bridge which was replaced by a handsome three-arched bridge. In the middle of the eighteenth century a fine road bridge was built at Penwortham, itself now redundant. Then came the tramroad, part of it now a footbridge crossing Avenham Park, which reminds us of the heyday of canal transport. From it one can see the railway bridges which were

Tram bridge, Preston

North Union Railway Bridge

built when Preston was developing and its population growing.

The earliest of the railway bridges over the Ribble at Preston was that of the North Union Railway Company. On 1 September 1835 the foundation stone was laid but two years later delays to further work were causing anxiety. In June 1837 it was decided to press the contractors to erect at once the five centres for the bridge. Four months later however there was a very serious setback; about ninety feet of culvert suddenly collapsed. A river was completely dammed and heavy rains on the following two days caused a rise of thirty feet in the water level. This in turn caused the embankment to collapse and a great quantity of earth was washed away. When that difficulty had been dealt with progress was good. By April 1838 it was reported that between 120 and 130 men including 40 masons were at work on the bridge and that three arches were almost complete. When finished the bridge was 872 feet long, 28 feet wide and 68 feet high from the river to the top of the parapet. The cost of the bridge was £40,000. It had five elliptical arches of 120 foot span, the piers were twenty feet thick and 22 feet high above the foundations. Altogether 675,000 cubic feet of rusticated ashlar was used, the material coming from Lancaster, Whittle and Longridge, so that local material was used.

The bridge was designed by Charles Vignoles and was modelled on the famous Waterloo Bridge in London. The later widening of the bridge means that it is not now possible to see the

East Lancashire Railway Bridge

graceful structure designed by Vignoles. When it was built the bridge, along with its adjoining embankments, was an enormous undertaking and throughout the nineteenth century was regarded as one of the finest and most substantial bridges in Britain.

Later in the century the bridge was strengthened and widened. In 1877 the first of the piles which supported the centring of the five new arches was driven, there were 600 piles. And in 1879 the last arch was keyed in. In 1896 permission was obtained to widen the bridge, the design being two double-track lattice girder spans which were to be placed alongside the original stone spans. Less graceful than stone, the iron work was probably cheaper. In 1904 the new bridge was brought into use.

The East Lancashire Railway Bridge marks the division between two of Preston's parks, Avenham Park and Miller Park. The original intention of the company was to build an embankment to take the line across the meadows at the approach to the river but when the contract was let, in November 1848 it included the construction of a viaduct. This was to consist of 52 brick arches each spanning 30 feet, each pier of the viaduct stood on 17 twelve-inch-square beech piles. The actual bridge over the river consisted of two brick arches of 25 foot span and three cast iron spans of 100 feet. These contained 520 tons of iron and were supplied by Joseph Butler and Company of Stanningley, near Leeds. When the line was inspected the girders were found to deflect only one quarter inch under a load of 200 tons. The opening was delayed by the collapse of thirteen arches of the viaduct on 25 October 1849 as the result of severe floods. In 1884-86 the viaduct was filled in and an embankment formed and in 1930 the cast iron girders were replaced by steel.

Attempts had been made in the 1840s to link Preston with Southport by rail but these attempts had come to nothing. In 1870 the project was revived when a group of wealthy Southport residents promoted a company to build the railway. In May 1870 the Preston and Southport Railway Bill came before a Select Committee of the House of Commons and was opposed by two existing railway companies, the London and North Western and the Lancashire and Yorkshire. The Bill did however progress to the House of Lords but was defeated.

The Company made renewed application the following year and used the title West Lancashire Railway. The Bill was successful. The line was carried over the Ribble at Preston at a height of forty-five feet on a bridge of five sixty-foot iron spans which rested on piers of Longridge stone. At each end there was one land span and, to the north, a stone viaduct of twelve arches. The total length of this bridge, with its land spans and viaduct, was 900 feet.

The line of the West Lancashire Railway had twenty-two bridges between Preston and Hesketh Bank, that over the Ribble was one of the biggest and most important: another important one was that over the River Douglas at Hesketh Bank. The Douglas Bridge was to have four fixed spans and two opening spans of 30 feet each which would give a headway of twelve feet at high water. The swing bridge over the River Douglas was built on 24 cylindrical piles each of which was sunk twenty feet into the bed of the river and filled, as far as high water level, with concrete. The group of cylinders which was in the centre formed a protective circle for the swing span and wooden fenders were built to protect the piers.

It is interesting to note the type of building materials used in the construction of these bridges. In the East Lancashire line, as well as that of the West Lancashire Company and the NUR bridge across the Ribble, traditional materials, wood, stone and brick were used for most of the construction work along with some iron. In the Douglas Bridge a much greater proportion of metal was used as well as concrete which was a newer material.

Iron, and later steel, were having increasing use, along with traditional building materials stone and brick, in bridge building. Between Accrington and Burnley the Leeds and Liverpool Canal was crossed twice by bridges of wrought iron tubular girders which were later replaced by plate girder spans. A road near Haslingden was crossed by a bridge consisting of wrought iron tubular girders built by W. Fairbairn, and another of Fairbairn's tubular girder bridges with an 81-foot span went over the road at Langho.

The York-Scarborough line crossed the River Ouse by what has been described as a 'Noble Bridge'.[4] The width of the river at that point is 148 feet. The foundations of this bridge rested on cast iron piles 30 feet in length; 28 of these sustaining the centre pier which was of masonry of Bramley stone – Bramley stone quarries are near Leeds so that the stone was fairly local – filled in with brick. This pier alone contained 600 tons of stone. The side piers were of the same material, each was 30 feet wide and they were connected together, in lieu of arches, by two cast iron girders of 75 foot span each giving ample space for four or five river craft to pass under the bridge at once. There were eight of these girders each of which weighed about 28 tons so that including the foundations the bridge contained upwards of 230 tons of metal. The bridge was supported on either side of the river by a viaduct and embankment. The abutments stood on brick piles 35 feet deep and the centre pier and abutments were ornamented with a cornice and battlement of stone whilst the girders were surmounted by balustrades of wrought iron. The height of the centre pier was 45½ feet above the bed of the river.

In the East Riding of Yorkshire the railway which went from Hull to Barnsley was a latecomer on the railway scene, not getting its Act of authorisation until 1880. This was not the only difference between it and other railway companies further west. Brick, rather than stone, was used in the construction of many of the over bridges and also for the abutments of the underbridges of which there were a great many. The decision was taken to route the line on an embankment through much of the Hull area, a decision which resulted in the need for many underbridges. There were 35 within the Hull city boundary. Almost all the other railways, apart from that from Goole to Selby, were there already and the process of crossing them needed even more underbridges.

A stipulation of the 1880 Act was that the bridge over Beverley

Road must be 'of an ornamental design to be approved by the Corporation and the piers and abutments to be parallel with the road'. The parapet was of iron, quite elaborately designed and this was supported by brackets. There was ornamentation of fish scales on the bridge and in the centre above the main beam was the device of the Corporation in relief.

The bridge over Hedon Road in Hull, that over the NE railway at Eastrington and over the Midland Railway at Cudworth were of the plate girder type. A lattice girder type was also used and this was the type used on the Cannon Street and Neptune Street branches of the line where they crossed the NE Railway. There were two swing bridges over the River Hull and the River Ouse. These were designed by William Shelford who was the engineer to the line after he had been to France and Germany to look at swing bridges there. It is possible that there were some points of design in the swing bridges on the Hull and Barnsley Railway which were the result of his experience on the Continental trip. Both the Hull and the Ouse bridges had wrought iron lattice spans rather than plate girder spans. This looked much more graceful and had the additional, more practical quality of being lighter in weight, even so the swinging span of the Ouse Bridge weighed 649 tons. One of the disadvantages of the lightness was the loss in rigidity but this could be corrected by other means. The span on the Ouse was 248 feet and that on the Hull 131 feet.

Most of the railways in Yorkshire and Lancashire were built round, through or at the edge of the Pennines, hills which are deeply dissected by valleys. In the early days of cross-country transport the valleys and streams were bridged very high where the narrow turbulent water could be crossed by a single span packhorse type bridge. Railways had to be built to negotiate the lower reaches of these valleys as well as the wider river valleys which had not been used by packhorse traffic and so there was a need for many embankments and viaducts. Railways, like the roads and canals which preceded them, crossed the hills and so tunnels were necessary.

Timber was used a great deal for viaduct-building, sometimes as a temporary measure for centring the arch until a stone viaduct was completed, or the timber framework was filled in with an embankment, and sometimes intended as a permanent feature. The East Lancashire Line after negotiating a 1,302-foot tunnel was taken over Rishton reservoir on a viaduct which consisted of eighteen twelve-foot spans resting on timber piles. The Aspen valley was crossed by a huge timber viaduct, built for single-line traffic only, with 33 twenty-five foot spans resting on a platform of timber supported on piles and with a maximum height of seventy feet. Timber was necessary in this instance as the ground, which consisted of alternate layers of sand and soft bluish clay, did not offer a firm enough foundation for masonry piers. Both these timber viaducts were later filled in with embankments. In the building of the Primrose viaduct south of Clitheroe there were seven stone arches and one timber span of 120 feet. It needed 6,730 cubic feet of timber, 63,000 cubic feet of stone, twenty tons of cast and wrought iron and cost about £7,000. In 1869-70 the timber span was replaced by three stone arches. The East Lancashire Railway crossed the River Irwell by the Alderbottom viaduct of six timber spans.

Timber was used elsewhere on a more permanent basis with, in some cases, unpleasant results. At Denby Dale it had been intended to build a stone viaduct but at the time construction was about to begin there was a strike of masons and the engineer, John Hawkshaw, was compelled to make alternative plans. He designed a timber trestle viaduct which, during building, suffered considerable gale damage – on 27 January 1847. In February, the *Sheffield Iris* reported that,

> out of 50 perpendicular supports 27 have been blown down, and such was the distance they had to fall (100 feet) that the strongest timbers were broken into splinters and matchwood. This accident will occasion a further delay in the opening of the line and will be a serious loss to the contractors. The damage is estimated at about £5,000. The structure altogether has such a cobweb appearance and is so unsuitable for the place and purpose intended that the public generally are well satisfied with its fall. It is to be hoped that with this practical proof of the unsuitability of a wood viaduct the directors will adopt the original plan and build a stone one.[5]

Work, however continued on the timber structure and it was completed in the following year. Standing 112 feet high and built on a curve and having a gradient of one in 200 rising towards Penistone, there were two stone spans at the north end of 40 and 56 feet and a timber section of 56 fifteen foot openings.

Mytholmbridge viaduct over New Mill Dyke was also built of timber. Like that at Denby Dale it had been originally decided to build it of stone but again and for different reasons Hawkshaw had to use timber. This time it was a question of simple economics, timber being cheaper than stone. It was smaller than the Denby Dale viaduct and of a different design. It consisted of 26 bays, each measuring 26 feet six inches. It had a maximum height of 86 feet six inches. However events took a common turn with the viaduct at Denby Dale, for on 19 February 1849 when it was almost finished, a great gale suddenly sprang up and at 12.30 p.m. almost three-quarters of the viaduct fell down. It was fortunate that all the workmen were at lunch and so there were no casualties. This collapse of the trestles was no doubt accompanied by a collapse of public confidence. However work started again and the viaduct was completed, although many people were so terrified at the danger of timber viaducts that they refused to travel over them. In July 1851 the Lancashire and Yorkshire Railway Company asked Robert Stephenson to examine the viaduct hoping that his reply would allay the fears of the travelling public. In his reply he stated 'It affords me satisfaction to be able to report to you my entire conviction of their perfect safety. Their strength is abundant and I consider their mode of construction simple and efficient … you may rest assured that both structures are perfectly safe and only require careful and periodical examination by your resident engineer who should from time to time make reports upon them to the Board.'[6]

On 21 April 1855 the timber viaduct at Horbury caught fire and so in May the executive committee recorded that a yearly report was to be submitted on all wooden viaducts especially on the Penistone and Holmfirth Lines. The Lancashire and Yorkshire Railway Company was aware that the timber viaducts would, sooner or later, have to be replaced. In the early 1860s designs for stone structures were prepared and in 1864 the tender of Henry Wadsworth was accepted for the reconstruction of the Mytholmbridge viaduct.

The new stone viaduct consisted of thirteen arches, two of 29 feet and the rest of a 37-foot-eight-inch span. The new stone work was erected on the inside of the curve formed by the timber viaduct and the piers were placed between the timber uprights. It seemed however that the viaduct was dogged by ill luck for as the new one neared completion cracks were noted in the seventh pier from the Huddersfield end and three buttresses were built to support it.

Early on the morning of 3 December 1865 there was a thunderous roar which reverberated through the valley. The entire viaduct was collapsing – the stone structure carrying with it the remaining part of the timber structure. Providentially there was a miller, a William England, who worked close to one end of the viaduct. He knew that a train was due very soon and so he dashed to the nearest station (no telephone boxes in those days), and managed to give warning in time to have the train stopped.

A report on the wreckage stated that it was possible that '... the failure has arisen from some unsoundness in the foundation of one of the piers'.[7] It would have taken at least a year to build another viaduct so it was suggested that instead an embankment should be built, this being quicker and less costly. But there was difficulty in obtaining sufficient land for an embankment and so instead it was decided to rebuild the viaduct at an estimated cost of £12,000.

In January 1866 the contractor, Wadsworth, revealed that the foundation of one of the piers, pier seven, was placed half on rock and half on gravel with the result that it had slipped out of place. It was decided at the enquiry that it was this, combined with bad workmanship which was the cause of the disaster. In March 1867 a new viaduct was opened.

People were becoming increasingly anxious about the safety of the Denby Dale viaduct and in November 1869 Huddersfield Town Council claimed that it was unsafe. There was an inspection and the viaduct was declared to be in a satisfactory condition. In April 1874 another inspection took place after which it was reported that the condition of the viaduct had deteriorated. Two years later, in July 1876 the building of a new viaduct and the demolition of the timber trestle were authorised and on 3 October 1877 a contract was signed for a new viaduct with costs set at £26,650. Trouble lay ahead for the railway company, some eighteen months later it was reported that there would be extra costs mainly because it was necessary to increase the depth of the foundations and build a retaining wall at the south end. These costs amounted to £10,697. On 16 May 1880 the new viaduct, consisting of 22 arches of various spans, was opened. Eighteen months later another inspection resulted in the viaduct being declared unsafe because of coal workings underneath. It was recommended that it should be underpinned at a cost of £15,000 and in the mean time a maximum speed of eight miles per hour was advised over the viaduct. Eventually matters were put right.

Another timber viaduct which came to a sad end was that at Horbury, where, the day before the opening was to take place, a cinder from an engine ignited some rubbish which the contractor had left between the old and the new parts and very soon the viaduct was ablaze. Six bays of the new portion were destroyed and damage to the extent of £500-£600 ensued which had to be made good by the contractor. In 1864-65 Horbury viaduct was rebuilt with iron spans on stone piers by Fairbairn Engineering Company.

Timber trestles were erected for the purposes of providing a framework for a stone viaduct, such a one was at Conisborough. Here some 40,000 cubic feet of timber was used, this had previously been used in the erection of the King Edward VII bridge at Newcastle. The Conisborough viaduct was built in red brick faced with blue bricks and, in its construction twelve million bricks and 3,000 tons of cement were used. It was of double-track width, level and straight; its length was 1,525 feet and its height above the river Don 113 feet. It had 21 arches of 55 foot span.

There are many more viaducts on the railways of Yorkshire

Lockwood viaduct

and Lancashire, some now disused, others still in use and built from one of the traditional building materials of brick or stone or a combination of the two, and sometimes using iron as well. Some of the viaducts, were, relatively early in the history of their particular railway, filled in and converted to embankments. That

Gauxholme viaduct

Nott Wood viaduct

at Holme, in the Cliviger valley, was converted to an embankment in 1886 and at Wakefield there was a viaduct of sixteen arches which was filled in to form an embankment in 1901.

The viaduct at Church, near Accrington, was of seven 40 foot span brick arches 50 feet high while that at Accrington consisted of 21 brick arches each of 40 foot span. The viaduct stood on a curve and its maximum height was 60 feet. During the construction of the viaduct at Accrington four piers began to sink and had to be demolished and rebuilt. In 1866 it again became unsafe and on 4 July the engineer reported that £11,215 would be needed to reconstruct it. By September 1867 this work was reported finished. There was a need to build more viaducts as the East Lancashire line progressed further east; at Burnley Bank Top the line crossed a viaduct of fifteen stone spans, at Marsden there was a brick viaduct of five 40-foot spans 50 feet high and at Colne there was another of six stone spans.

There were many viaducts crossing the Calder Valley; that at Charlestown near Todmorden consisted of three stone spans over the roadway and a cast iron span over the canal, the viaduct was altered in the 1940s. At Copley the railway line crossed the Calder Valley by a viaduct of 23 arches at a height of 66 feet over the river. The spans varied from 70 feet to 40 feet with an arch over the road of 51 feet four inch span and a rise of only seven feet. A very fine stone viaduct crossed the centre of Todmorden town while further up the Walsden valley just before the beginning of Summit tunnel stood Gauxholme viaduct. This consisted of an iron span over the Rochdale Canal, seventeen stone spans of 35 feet and one of 60 feet over the river. Just beyond this the canal was crossed again at a height of 40 feet by a handsome skew bridge of 101-foot span with two stone turrets at each end. One of the most picturesque settings for a viaduct is that at Nott Wood in the Cliviger valley between Todmorden and Burnley.

There are several stone viaducts in the Colne valley, notably a fine erection at Slaithwaite and in the Huddersfield area were more spectacular viaducts. One was at Paddock and consisted of six stone spans, four spans of 77 feet each formed of six wrought iron lattice girders seven feet deep and built as continuous beams 345 feet long and also another nine stone spans. The viaduct was built on a curve. The ironwork cost £5,175.

More famous is the Lockwood viaduct. The stone was all obtained from the two cuttings immediately to the south of it from which altogether 5,452,650 cubic feet were removed. The total length of the viaduct was 1,428 feet and the greatest height from the base of the foundations to the top of the parapet 136 feet. The rails were taken over the river at a height of 122 feet. The viaduct consisted of 32 semi-circular arches of 30 foot span with an oblique arch of 70 foot span over the Meltham road and another of 42 foot span over a road at the south end. All the piers were the same thickness four foot six inches at the springing of the arches and had a batter of one sixth of an inch per foot. The viaduct used some 972,000 cubic feet of masonry in its

Huddersfield Loco Bridge, Turnbridge

construction and was built in a style of masonry known as 'snecked rubble' which was unusual at the time it was built for work on such a large scale. Building began at the end of 1846 and was interrupted for long periods by difficulties both financial and connected with labour. By March 1849 there remained only the parapet to be added. The total cost of the viaduct was £33,000.

The building of the viaduct at Huddersfield itself was a very big task. Built at a cost of £48,000 it was 1989 feet long and comprised 45 stone spans and two iron spans over the streets, and rose to a maximum height of 53 feet. About half the viaduct from the north end to the Bradford Road was built for two tracks while the remainder was built for four tracks. Later the viaduct was enlarged to take five tracks. The difficulty of the terrain through which the Yorkshire railway builders had to build their lines is obvious when one realises that thirteen miles of track between Huddersfield and Penistone involved the boring of six tunnels, totalling 10,281 feet and the building of four major viaducts in addition to deep cuttings, immense embankments and 30 bridges.

An undertaking of similar magnitude was the building of the Oaks viaduct at Barnsley which was 1,087 feet long and eventually spanned two railways, a main road, the River Dearne, the Dearne and Dove canal and the Barnsley canal.

The Penistone viaduct had 29 arches of 30 foot span built on a curve which took the line 98 feet above the river. The viaduct had an extreme length of 1,100 feet and in building it John Hawkshaw used the 'block in course' construction, a method which he described as 'requiring great care in execution'. Basically it consisted of an outside wall of rough faced ashlar with stones averaging twelve inches thick and fifteen to eighteen inches on the bed and filling the interior with rubble masonry.

At Whalley there was a viaduct of 48 spans, 2,037 feet long and 70 feet above the River Calder. This used seven million bricks and 436,000 cubic feet of stone and cost £35,000. About 10,000 feet of timber were needed for piles platforms and centres. Viewed from the road bridge and from the top of the hill on the Blackburn road this look extremely impressive. Another Lancashire viaduct was that near Gisburn where the Stock Beck valley was crossed by a massive stone viaduct of eight 40-foot spans. It was 500 feet long standing 96 feet above the bed of the stream.

Viaducts enhance the landscape, particularly attractive are those at Healey Dell near Whitworth; at Wyke, between

Healey Dell viaduct

Huddersfield and Bradford, at Thornton, also near Bradford and at Hewenden near Cullingworth which was the highest structure on the Great Northern Railway and had a maximum height of 123 feet and its foundations were also the deepest. It was composed of seventeen arches each of 50 foot span and its length was 1,128 feet.

Perhaps the best known of the viaducts is that at Knaresborough which appears with predictable inevitability on almost every view of the town. The foundation stone was laid in April 1847 and the structure collapsed on March 11th 1848. It

Staithes viaduct

was rebuilt at a cost of £10,000, its length being 300 feet and the height 90 feet.

Railway viaducts are lofty rather than squat but they combine grace with solidity. Two, which give the impression of fragility and an altogether too slender aspect are two which were built by the Whitby, Redcar and Middlesbrough Union Railway. Both had lattice girder spans; one was on the last stretch of the Cleveland line which was opened in 1867. It was in fact the delay in completion of the viaduct which held back the line's opening. Spanning the Kilton Valley between Shinningrove and Loftus, it was 678 feet long and had twelve 45-foot lattice girder spans which were on masonry piers and, at their highest, were 150 feet above the stream. It was not however that the lattice girder piers were fragile – the stability of the viaduct became threatened by ore mine workings. The viaduct therefore was encased by an immense embankment.

Another viaduct whose stability was threatened also had a fragile appearance. This was near Staithes and was 700 feet long, 152 feet high at its maximum and had six 60-foot lattice girder spans which were supported on tubular iron columns in pairs filled with concrete and braced together. Eight years after the viaduct was built it was strengthened by the addition of two horizontal lattice bracings. It was in a very exposed position subject to batterings by gales and it was because of this that eventually a wind gauge was installed at one end. If the gales from the North Sea exceeded a certain velocity, the passage of trains across the viaduct was temporarily suspended.

The number of viaducts needed to cross the Pennine valleys was great, so too was the number of tunnels; the line from Bradford to Manchester seems to go in and out of tunnels much of the time. Some were built on a curve, others were straight and it is fascinating to watch the tiny pin-point of light grow bigger and bigger as the train nears the end of the tunnel.

The biggest undertaking on this line was Summit Tunnel between Todmorden and Littleborough. The spoil heaps from its building added to the existing hilly formation of the land make the hillside seem like a mountain. Work on the tunnel began in 1838; by March progress seemed so slow that another engineer was appointed. The tunnelling now went ahead at a rate of 450 feet per month but even with this rate of progress there was doubt about whether the tunnel would be ready for opening for the agreed date. In May 1840 a bonus scheme was started by which an extra day's wage was paid for every foot of progress which was made beyond the stipulated amount at any face. The work was heavy, unpleasant, and very dangerous. In September 1839 three men and two boys were killed in an accident. In January 1840 three more men were killed and another in May 1840.

There were other problems apart from the physical ones of hewing the rock and lining the face; there was dissatisfaction among the bricklayers which led to a combination being formed. Their rates of pay were six shillings and sixpence for a ten-hour day. Meanwhile costs were mounting; building operations taking more time than had originally been bargained for. By the end of March 1840 the original estimate of cost had been exceeded. However in December of that year the last brick was keyed in. At the time of its completion Summit Tunnel was the longest in the world being 8,655 feet long. In the course of construction 23 million bricks and 8,000 tons of Roman cement were used. The cost of the tunnel was £251,000.

Woodhead Tunnel, which connected Sheffield and Manchester and was 3 miles 66 feet long was opened in December 1845. It was the longest tunnel in the country at the time of its opening. The

Standedge railway tunnel, Marsden

Sheffield Iris described it as a 'wondrous triumph of art over nature'.[8] Like the tunnel at Summit it too cost more than the amount which was originally estimated, some £200,000 compared with the initial estimate of £60,000. About 157 tons of gunpowder were used in blasting the rock during the course of its construction. Like the tunnel at Summit there was a great human toll, 26 lives were lost and 140 navvies were injured.

Less than a year after it opened, it was realised a single bore was inadequate to carry the volume of traffic so in February 1847 the contract for a second tunnel was let. This time more attention was paid to the welfare of the navvies and their families who were working on the tunnel; in 1848 a school for the children of the workpeople was established. In February 1852 the new line came into use.

Like the tunnels at Summit and Woodhead, Standedge Tunnel was, when it opened, the longest in Britain and managed to retain this distinction for nearly forty years. It also shared common ground with its two great predecessors in that its actual cost greatly exceeded the original estimate, the estimate being £147,240 and the cost £201,608. The amount of candles used seems phenomenal, over 150,000 pounds costing £3,618.

Like Woodhead the tunnel was a single bore, and again like

Bramhope tunnel

Woodhead this was not found to be adequate and so a second bore was started in 1868 and completed in February 1871.

Another tunnel which was costly in terms of loss of life was that at Bramhope between Leeds and Otley on the Leeds to Thirsk railway line. The terrain, in Lower Wharfedale, is altogether softer than the wild bleak countryside at the head of Ribblesdale but there were nevertheless great hazards. The tunnel, which was 2 miles 723 feet long was constructed through sand and shale. It is said this was longer than engineering requirements demanded but was necessary in order to meet the wishes of a landowner through whose estates the line passed. It was carried over the river by 21 arches each of 60-foot span. Water caused great problems during the building of the tunnel, in fact, 1,563,480,000 gallons had to be pumped out. During the building of the tunnel some 20 working shafts were sunk sometimes as deep as 280 feet below the surface of Otley Chevin. A memorial to the many who lost their lives in the process of the tunnel's construction was built in Otley churchyard, built in the shape of the tunnel portal. The tunnel was also costly financially.

About the time the second Standedge tunnel bore was being worked, a completely new venture began, a venture which in terms of railway history was late off the ground. This was the construction, by the Midland Railway Company, of a line to Scotland, a line which later events, or lack of events, have probably made the most famous line in the country, that from Settle to Carlisle.

The construction of 73 miles of line, reaching at its summit a height of 1,169 feet has been referred to as 'the crowning triumph of British Railroad genius'.[9] And yet the initial reaction to the projected line was not favourable. When the ground was first surveyed at least one engineer thought that the territory was unsafe and impracticable for railway building. There would, he was sure, be a need to divert public ways, in at least one place the river would have to be crossed. The whole project, he maintained, needing as it did secure foundations for nearly a score of viaducts as well as vast amounts of boring and blasting through the hardest rock, including many miles of tunnelling, was just too immense. Even if a railway could be built, the rails would be placed at such a high altitude that they would be liable to the dangers of sudden waterspouts and floods and in winter to repeated and impassable drifts of snow.

But the project went ahead and the navvies faced all the tedium and unpleasantness of working conditions which had been endured by those who had worked on the tunnels at Summit, Woodhead, Standedge, Bramhope, and the smaller tunnels which cut through the Pennines. But nowhere in the South Pennines is the terrain as tough as in the region of the Three Peaks, with the boggy peat hags, the large tussocks of grass, the exposed treeless moor where ferocious winds tear the soul out of you and where, in winter, the snow piles up in deep drifts. It has too its gentle side, pleasant grassy patches and limestone outcrops which shine and sparkle when the sun touches them.

Towards the end of 1869, plans were sufficiently advanced for the railway company to be able to contract for the construction work and the area was divided into five sections let under five separate contracts. Contract number one was the stretch of territory between Settle Junction and Dent Head. On this section nearly 3,000 labourers were employed. It was the toughest section of the whole line reaching in Blea Moor Tunnel an altitude of 1,151 feet. This tunnel is 7,920 feet long and, in the deepest part 500 feet below the outer surface. The work of boring and clearing was extremely unpleasant and dangerous. During its construction there was a great waterspout on Whernside which inundated the tunnel and did immense damage, such great damage that many people thought it would have to be abandoned as a hopeless job. While it was in progress about £50 per month was spent on candles to give light for the men to work.

The great viaduct at Batty Green, later re-named the Ribblehead viaduct was a prodigious piece of engineering. It contained 918,000 cubic feet of masonry besides 6,000 feet of concrete. Its length was 1,328 feet, and it had 24 arches with an average span of 45 feet and the height of the highest from the parapet to the foundations was 165 feet. Nearly all the piers rested on a bed of concrete six feet thick, laid upon the solid rock. They were thirteen feet thick at the base and six feet at the spring of the arch; every sixth pier was partly for ornament, but chiefly as a means of increasing the strength and was eighteen feet thick at the top instead of six. The entire line included nineteen viaducts, thirteen tunnels and many miles of embankments and cuttings.

The railway company budgeted, in terms of money, £2,200,000 for the cost of the line and four years in terms of time. The first sod was cut in November 1869. The line was officially opened for freight traffic in August 1875, and for passenger traffic on 1 May 1876. The cost, was, as announced in 1876, expected to be £3,467,000 working out at a figure of £47,500 per mile. Many of the bigger works, Ribblehead viaduct, Blea Moor tunnel, Rise Hill tunnel and Smardale viaduct, took four or five years to complete. Dynamite costing £200 a ton was used in the construction of the tunnels.

Much of the stone used in the building of the viaducts, bridges, tunnels and culverts was quarried locally. Transporting large quantities of stone from any distance over such rough terrain would have added enormously to the expense of the line. Some of

Ribblehead viaduct

the tunnels, even though they were driven through solid rock had to be supported. In Rise Hill tunnel, wrought iron supporting ribs were used to reinforce the limestone strata. Various means were used to carry material for supporting and lining the tunnels and building the viaducts: narrow gauge tramways, trains of packhorses – except that they were donkeys – and a unique bog cart which was a contraption with the body of a cart and shaft on a revolving barrel instead of wheels, was used to negotiate the boggy peat hags.

On several occasions the drifts of snow on the line were tremendous. On 27 October 1880 there was a depth of ten to fifteen feet and at Dent Head in December 1882 a force of 700 men was despatched from Leeds and Carlisle to clear the line for some miles before traffic could be resumed. Conditions like these would no doubt prevail during some of the winters when the line was being constructed.

The navvies lived mainly in encampments of huts at various points along the track. The biggest and most famous was that at Batty Wife Hole later re-named Batty Green, located near the site of the present Ribblehead station. The men lived in huts which were built in rows. The settlement was similar to a town having a school, post office, library and mission house.

The households seem to have been of varying sizes, some having as few as three members, others having as many as seven, eight or nine or even more. The larger huts contained a natural family and also a varying number of lodgers. The navvies came from all parts of the British Isles and the settlement in huts may have been of groups of people who came to the area together or made up willy nilly from single individuals needing a home. One hut accommodated a man, wife, two sons and five lodgers, all from Wales but the lodgers from different parts of the Principality. Another, of man and wife and five lodgers had a mix, the lodgers coming from Warwickshire, Yorkshire, Devonshire, Oxfordshire and Scotland. Those stated were the places of their birth. Navvying work was by nature undertaken by itinerant workmen, the 'group' may have met up elsewhere and stayed together. Certainly the labour force was drawn from men born in all parts of the British Isles; Northamptonshire, Derbyshire, Lancashire, Scotland, Suffolk, Gloucestershire, Shropshire, Norfolk, many of the counties one does not associate with the kind of rough work needed on a railway line. Their occupations are various; many are listed as labourers, but there were also miners, blacksmiths, engine-driver, horse-driver, quarryman, smith, engineer, nurse, civil engineer.

A standard railway bridge resembles a standard canal bridge, with a single arch, a parapet with buttresses at either side, wing walls and a single string course, or perhaps two string courses, between the arch and the parapet. Such a bridge is that at the east end of Howden station.

Many of the tunnel ends are similar (a tunnel is, after all, an elongated bridge) but on some the builder used more elaborate designs. On the line between Bradford and Todmorden where there are a great many tunnels, each has its own individuality. On some the arch stones are cut to a point in a zigzag pattern; on one a roll-moulding surmounting a stepped edge; another has a string course round the arch; another a thick bulging surround about twelve inches wide, this has a plain edge but yet another has an arch surround with a scalloped edge. On another the arch stones and the spandrel are merged in diagonally placed stones.

The penchant for a revival of medieval styles affected not only station architecture but also tunnel ends. The western end of the tunnel just outside Halifax station has a cornice of small rounded arches and the tunnel mouth consists of two recessed arches

Halifax tunnel

decorated with 'Norman' moulding, rather reminiscent of a church porch.

A tunnel entrance near Sowerby Bridge station, now disused, is like the gatehouse of a castle with the mouth of the tunnel flanked on each side by a high battlemented tower. This is very similar to the ornamental south portal of the 468-foot-long Gisburn tunnel which carries the Hellifield-Blackburn line underneath the park.

One of the most splendid, if indeed splendid is the most appropriate word, tunnel entrances is that at the northern end of the Bramhope tunnel. The entrance is flanked by two round towers in the style of later medieval castles, one rather bigger than the other. There are battlements and slits for arrows, as if the tunnel was in imminent danger of attack. The parapet of the tunnel is also battlemented and there is another small tower at the end of the wing wall. Gauxholme viaduct near Todmorden is similarly adorned in psuedo-medieval splendour.

North Bridge, Halifax, which has some ornate iron work is 'guarded' at either end and at each side by square battlemented towers, each a double tower, eight in all and with late medieval embellishments. There is ball flower, stylised foliage as well as animal gargoyles.

The west end of the tunnel at South Kirkby is very pleasing having a cornice with denticles and two narrow string courses below it. There are buttresses at either side of the tunnel. The arch has a distinctive roll moulding and two more finely cut narrow edges lower down which give the impression of slightly recessed arches. It is a fine substantial structure with a bold, prominent and distinctive keystone.

6 Mason Marks

Many of the early canal bridges were built by small firms which were based in the immediate locality of a particular section of canal construction. In the later years of canal building and during the railway age bridges and viaducts were built by big contracting firms. Large contracting of this nature was a new feature of the late eighteenth and early nineteenth centuries, and yet in another sense there was nothing new about it: in the Middle Ages the monasteries operated large business enterprises including contracting. The monastic houses owned or leased large quarries from which they obtained stone to build their monasteries, churches and cathedrals, and, just as importantly for the continuance of their secular enterprises, bridges. A master mason was appointed by the monastery and his position was not unlike that of a bailiff on an agricultural estate. It was his business to see that the building work, as requisitioned by the monastic authorities, was carried out, and he would prepare estimates of cost, make contracts, buy materials and submit accounts. He employed a variety of worker, master masons, rough masons, apprentices, quarrymen and labourers, the masons and apprentices living in a lodge which consisted of several rooms or buildings on the site of their work.

Mason work was a craft, which, like other crafts in the Middle Ages, had strict rules guiding its practice. Boys apprenticed to it had to obey their master and promise not to reveal the mysteries of the craft to outsiders. Masters on their part undertook to teach the apprentices, to feed, house and discipline them. Apprenticeship was for seven years at the end of which time the boys had to pass a test qualifying them as journeymen craftsmen. Rough masons worked in walling and plain stone building, and free masons had the added skill of stone carving and working in free stone – any type of stone which could be cut and carved. One of

161

the distinguishing features between a rough mason and a free mason was that the latter worked with a chisel.

During the Middle Ages the monastic masons carried out the building work needed by the monasteries but occasionally they were available for secular work; one example of this being the building of Tadcaster bridge when the body of master masons attached to Healaugh Priory, the canons having finished with their services for the time being, were employed on the building of the bridge.

When the monasteries were dissolved in the sixteenth century large numbers of masons who had been employed by them found themselves at liberty to take what employment they could find. They formed lodges or groups and undertook building work of a secular nature where it was needed. The lodges maintained the rules and regulations of the crafts, often the groups contained a master mason who was the lodge master. The medieval guilds were dissolved by Edward VI and it is interesting to note that the free masons guild flourished until modern times, although modern freemasonry has nothing to do with stone cutting.

Marking a product as a guarantee of standard and quality and also as some proof of origin was common in the Middle Ages and the craft of masonry was no exception. The marker, or bench marks, which can be found on stones are thought to be the personal trade mark of an individual mason who cut the stones at the bench, as on his election as a free mason he was entitled to adopt a mark. It has been suggested that there was a central register of mason marks, or, that the master mason in charge of every new building distributed marks to the masons as he employed them. Many of the more common marks however are duplicated so it seems unlikely that a mason distributed fresh marks with every new building.

The most straightforward assumption is that masons chose their own mark more or less haphazardly, each man selecting according to his own pleasure. As with surnames some marks are common and others are rare. Some, though by no means all, masons, adopted the mark of their father or master and made a slight alteration to it.

A Mr Brown who worked at Chatsworth at some time during the nineteenth century is reported to have had a book in which were hundreds of marks with the names of the masons and stonecutters alongside. As a new hand or craftsman was put on a job he added an additional nick or score to his master's or foreman's mark so that at once every man's work was known by his mark. A mason from Yorkshire, at the end of his apprenticeship, when his master was dead, stated that he assumed his mark, while a Lancashire mason said he gave up his own mark and assumed that of his father when his father died.[1]

It is possible that a mason mark was some way of keeping

Croston Bridge

check on the work of a particular man and that in the early days men were required by authority to mark their stone rather than doing it as a matter of pride in their work. It has been suggested that an apprentice could possess a mark as his personal property, although whether, during his apprenticeship, he was permitted to mark the stones he prepared, is not clear. This is somewhat at variance with the theory that it was at his election as a free mason that a man was entitled to adopt a mark.

It was customary to cut the mark in the middle, or as near the middle as possible of the stone face so that it could be easily seen when the stone was placed in the wall. Some masons carefully cut their mark in the straight position but others did not. Often the mark was cut as the mason happened to be standing when the stone was finished and as a result marks appear to be the wrong way up. Not all stones are marked therefore it may be that the better workmen were not required to sign their stones.

Many of the marks which are apparent on the road and canal bridges in Yorkshire and Lancashire have been crudely cut. This, along with the fact that not all the stones bear mason marks, lends weight to the theory that it was perhaps the less able workmen, or the casual and largely unknown workmen who were required to mark their stones, thus giving the master mason opportunity to check on their work. Many of the marks are wrongside up or sideways on. Many are duplicated, A's and W's being common. The existence of ✗ and ∀ and ∀ on Airton bridge may have meant that there were three first generation masons who all had a name beginning with A; or that a second or third generation mason had added a notch to the mark of his forebears. The marks at Barden seem the most likely to have been done by second or third generation masons.

Masons were not necessarily literate and their unfamiliarity with the printed word could lead to serious, or amusing situations. At Goosenargh in 1819 a bridge was built at Whinney Clough which was washed down in 1858. Another bridge was built in that year with the inscription,

It should, of course, have read,

AD 1858
1 JBR S

The mason was more at home with the chisel than the pen and so the inscription was written for him. On turning the paper face down he produced the first version.

Mason Marks (Road Bridges)

THORP ARCH	(mason marks)
BOLTON, near Bolton Priory	(mason marks)
SMALL BRIDGE, nr Bolton Bridge	(mason marks)
ILKLEY OLD	(mason marks)
COTTINGLEY	(mason marks)
TADCASTER	(mason marks)
	(mason marks)
SETTLE	(mason marks)
WHALLEY	(mason marks)
CATTERICK	(mason marks)
LINTON	(mason marks)
BARDEN	(mason marks)
AIRTON	(mason marks)

Mason Marks (Canal Bridges)

Telford's mark on Langholm Brig, across the Esk in Dumfriesshire

	Marks
LANCASTER	(mason marks)
CALDER and HEBBLE	(mason marks)
HUDDERSFIELD BROAD	(mason marks)
HUDDERSFIELD NARROW	(mason marks)
LEEDS and LIVERPOOL	(mason marks)
ROCHDALE	(mason marks)

Notes

Chapter 1

[1] Samuel Smiles, *Lives of the Engineers*, Vol. 3, 1904
[2] Phyllis Whitehead, *The Brontës came here*, n.d.
[3] Quoted in W.B. Crump, *Huddersfield Highways Down the Ages*, 1968 edn.
[4] Quoted in J. Blakey, *Stories and Annals of Old Barrowford*, 1929
[5] Quoted in H. Speight, *Chronicles and Stories of Old Bingley*, 1898

Chapter 2

[1] J.J. Brigg, *The King's highway in Craven*, 1927
[2] Surtees Society, Vol. 53, 1868
[3] Surtees Society, Vol. 53, 1868
[4] Surtees Society, Vol. 30, 1855
[5] Surtees Society, Vol. 45, 1864
[6] Lancashire and Cheshire Antiquarian Society, Vol. V, 1887
[7] Historic Society of Lancashire and Cheshire, Vol. 98, 1946
[8] Quoted in Fred Cobley, *Upper and Lower Wharfedale*, 1890
[9] Yorkshire Archaeological Society Record Series, Vol. 2, Quoted in H. Speight, *Craven and N.W. Yorkshire Highlands*, 1892
[10] Transactions Halifax Antiquarian Society, 1915
[11] W.B. Crump, *Ancient Highways of Halifax*, Reprinted from Halifax Antiquarian Society Papers, 1924-28
[12] W.B. Crump, *Ancient Highways of Halifax*, ditto
[13] W.B. Crump, *Ancient Highways of Halifax*, ditto
[14] A. Raistrick, *Yorkshire Dalesman* No. 6, Vol. 3, Sept. 1941
[15] Quoted in A. Raistrick, *Yorkshire Dalesman* No.6, Vol. 3, Sept 1941
[16] Halifax Local Portfolio, No. LVII, Aug. 29 1857
[17] As 16
[18] Yorkshire Archaeological Society Journal, Vol. 30, 1930-31
[19] As 16
[20] As 16
[21] As 7
[22] As 7
[23] G.A. Cooke, *Topographical and Statistical Description of the County of Yorkshire*, 1818
[24] West Riding Book of Contracts, 18th cent.
[25] As 7
[26] Quoted in *Wakefield District Heritage*, Vol. 1, 1976

²⁷ Yorkshire Archaeological Society Record Series, Vol. XCIV, 1936
²⁸ W. Bennett, *The History of Marsden and Nelson*, 1957
²⁹ A. Young, *A 6 months Tour Through the North of England*, 4 Vols, 2nd edn, 1770-71
³⁰ As 28

Chapter 3

¹ Quoted in *British Bridges: an illustrated Technical and Historical record*, pub. Organising Committee of the Public Works Roads and Transport Congress, 1933
² North Riding Records, Quoted in H. Speight, *Romantic Richmondshire*, 1897
³ Rev. Thomas Parkinson, *Yorkshire Legends and Traditions*, 1888. The name Ferris is used by some authors.
⁴ Historic Society of Lancashire and Cheshire, Vol. 98, 1946
⁵ Henry Fishwick, *History of the Parish of Preston*, 1900
⁶ Rev. T.D. Whitaker, *History of Whalley*, 1818
⁷ As 4
⁸ Quoted in J. Walker, *Wakefield, its history and people*, 1934
⁹ Quoted in J.S. Fletcher, *A book about Yorkshire*, 1908
¹⁰ Quoted in A. Raistrick, *Yorkshire Dalesman* No. 6, Vol. 3, Sept. 1941
¹¹ H. Speight, *Lower Wharfedale*, 1902
¹² E. Bogg, *Lower Wharfeland, The Old City of York and the Ainsty*, 1904
¹³ As 9

Chapter 4

¹ J. Aiken, *A description of the country from 30-40 miles round Manchester*, 1795
² Charles Dickens, *Pickwick Papers*
³ Quoted in C.T.G. Boucher, *John Rennie*, 1963
⁴ *Blackburn Mail*, June 1803
⁵ *Wakefield Journal*, 16 August 1839

Chapter 5

¹ John Ruskin, *Seven Lamps of Architecture, The Lamp of Mercury*
² *Illustrated London News*, 3 November 1849
³ *Lancaster Gazette*, 2 July 1864
⁴ *The Tourists Companion on the History and Description of the scenes and places on the route by railway from York to Scarborough*, 2nd edn., 1846
⁵ Quoted in John Marshall, *The Lancashire and Yorkshire Railway*, Vol. 1, 1969
⁶ As 5
⁷ As 5
⁸ Quoted in David Joy, *The Railways of South and West Yorkshire*, 1975
⁹ F.W. Houghton and W. Hubert Foster, *The Story of the Settle to Carlisle Line*, 2nd edn., 1965

Chapter 6

[1] *Builder*, Vol. XVI, 1858
[2] Richard Cookson, *Goosenargh Past and Present*, 1887

Index